What An̲g̲ ̲ ̲ ̲

What Anglicans Believe

An Introduction

Samuel Wells

CANTERBURY
PRESS
Norwich

© Samuel Wells 2011

Published in 2011 by Canterbury Press
Fourth impression 2020
Editorial office
108–114 Golden Lane,
London, EC1Y 0TG, UK

Canterbury Press is an imprint of Hymns Ancient and Modern Ltd
(a registered charity)
13a Hellesdon Park Road, Norwich, Norfolk, NR6 5DR

www.canterburypress.co.uk

British Library Cataloguing in Publication data

A catalogue record for this book is available
from the British Library

978 1 84825 114 4

Typeset by Regent Typesetting, London
Printed and bound by
CPI Group (UK) Ltd, Croydon, CR0 4YY

Contents

For
Neville Black
Kate Litchfield
Andrew McKearney
Caroline Worsfold
Jean Yull

Preface

This book is written for anyone who wants to know more about the Church they don't belong to, wants to know more about the Church they belong to but don't always understand, or wants to know why they should continue to be a part of the Church given that they've become all too aware of its imperfections and, perhaps, their own.

One challenging aspect of writing the book has been what to call the members of this Church. Those who attend Church of England churches seldom call themselves 'Anglicans'. They would normally refer to themselves as 'Christians' or, if pushed, 'C of E'. In some cases they might prefer a more particular label, such as 'Evangelical' or 'Anglo-Catholic'. Other British Anglicans may also be reluctant to use 'Anglican' – in Scotland, for example, 'Episcopalian' is universally used. There is another problem with 'Anglican': in recent years it has been a way that groups in the USA, finding themselves in serious tension with The Episcopal Church, have nonetheless identified with the Anglican Communion as a whole, often by seeking oversight from a province in Africa or elsewhere.

Despite all these complications, 'Anglican' remains the only noun available to describe members of the Church of England and other provinces of the Anglican Communion (with the exception of those that have adopted the name 'Episcopalian'). I've used 'Anglican' in this book to refer to 'member of the Anglican Communion in its local manifestation, for example, member of the Church of England or Church in Wales'. When 'Anglican' appears as an adjective it isn't intended to signal a nod to any particular party within current controversies in the

USA or elsewhere, only to be a shorter and less cumbersome way of referring to the faith of the Anglican Communion as a whole. When I use the term 'Episcopal' (with a capital 'E') or 'The Episcopal Church' (the 'The' is part of the title), I am always referring to American Episcopalianism.

Duke Divinity School, though a United Methodist-affiliated institution, nonetheless has one of the strongest and most dynamic Episcopalian and Anglican faculties to be found anywhere, and it is a profound honour to be a part of it. It is especially rewarding to think about one's own tradition in the presence of and in conversation with such a diverse and vibrant collection of voices from other traditions. I am grateful to members of the Anglican Episcopal House of Studies and its director, Jo Bailey Wells, for giving me opportunities to think through these issues in a classroom setting.

Several people read and commented on all or part of the manuscript. Bill Gregg offered a marvellous and absorbing engagement with the whole text, with corrections, insights and challenges made all the more valuable for his dual vocation as a bishop of The Episcopal Church and a theologian. I have lost count of the ways his detailed and nuanced attention has improved my understanding and expression. Craig Uffman made a serious, scholarly and wide-ranging response to the project, and changed my mind on several questions. John Inge gave a helpful reading as a bishop from a Church of England perspective. Lisa Fischbeck and Abby Kocher also read drafts and made suggestions with wisdom and grace. Meanwhile Lauren Winner helped me understand American history more cogently. I am blessed to be able to draw on such colleagues and friends and to learn from them.

Rebekah Eklund has been a marvellous research assistant, finding and listing obscure sources, checking unusual details, correcting wayward manuscripts, patiently making thoughtful suggestions, and challenging overblown generalizations. She turns the burden of editing into a joy. My debt to her, in this and many other ventures, is beyond my calculation, and my gratitude is profound.

This book is dedicated to five Anglicans who show me what it means to be a part of God's Church, forgiven, loved, and free. They make me proud and grateful to be so. They also make me proud and grateful to know them and love them. My prayer is that readers of this book will be inspired to live lives like theirs.

Introduction

This is a book for the Church. It is for that part of the Church
known as the Anglican Communion and in different places by
local names, such as the Church of England or The Episcopal Church. It is written, initially, for a layperson who simply
would like to know what a member of such a Church would
normally believe. Such a layperson may be approaching confirmation, and for the first time taking seriously the contours of an
inherited faith. Or he or she may be coming from a different
branch of the universal Church – from Roman Catholicism,
perhaps, or from non-denominational Protestantism or from
another Christian denomination – and may be wondering in
what respects this Church differs from the one they already
know well. Or she or he may have grown up in another faith or
within no faith at all, and may now be more interested in what
Christians in general believe rather than the fine particulars of
how their beliefs differ.

So this book is designed for each one of these possible circumstances, but also for those who frequently encounter people
in these situations – teachers of the faith, in church, school
and college settings; clergy, seminary teachers; and all who are
looking for a straightforward, brief and accessible overview of
Christianity from within the Anglican and Episcopalian tradition. I have therefore tried simply to articulate the Christian
faith as seen in this broad tradition – not to locate myself within
a partisan catholic, liberal or evangelical stable, but to offer an
account that does justice to and may be welcomed by a wide
range of perspectives.

We live in controversial times – that is no new or unique experience. Christians have always differed about the theory and practice of their faith, and always will. Various themes make these current times *seem* more critical than any before them. These include the rapid changes in what can be done through applied technology, the immense power of weaponry that could wipe out huge populations at a stroke, and the climatic challenge to the ecological balance that threatens the long-term well-being of all earthly life. There is always a crisis looming somewhere and there will always be personalities who thrive on tension and interest groups that stand to benefit from portraying existing circumstances as potentially disastrous.

This book, by contrast, is not arguing that we live in especially momentous times. I believe that the key events in Christian history have already happened. These include the creation of the universe; the calling of and covenant with God's chosen people, the Jews; the incarnation, ministry, death, resurrection and ascension of Jesus; and the sending of the Holy Spirit. The first chapter of the book is therefore given over to describing what these events are and what they mean. One day the whole story will come to an end. But in the meantime, no event can compare in significance to these decisive episodes in the story of salvation. Every generation faces the challenge of bringing these central events face to face with the pressing issues of the day, and responding to these issues in ways that are faithful to the manner in which God has already been revealed. Indeed, one may go further and say that in every generation, God gives the Church opportunities to rediscover how abundant are the resources of the faith and how vibrant are the gifts of the Holy Spirit for meeting what would otherwise seem daunting trials.

Just at this moment there are intense debates in the Anglican Communion about sexuality. Compared to the tectonic shifts in the planet and its biosphere, humankind's relation to creation and the changes and damage we are capable of bringing upon one another, preoccupation with such issues may seem at best a displacement activity – at worst a wilful distraction. Nonetheless the debates are hard to ignore. Because there is so much concern about authority, I take time in the second chapter to consider it at some length. I don't doubt that the various approaches to current issues arise out of profound conviction, deep reflection and long-percolated wisdom. Yet I do hope that those on different sides of the debates who consider it is time for parts of the Church to 'walk apart' will review the description of the faith offered in these pages and ask themselves why, if we agree so substantially, it seems so necessary to part company. In short, if all parties can agree that this is their faith, can we not also see our need of one another?

It is often said that Anglicans have no doctrine. That is not, of course, true. The sentiment is intended either to indicate that we base our understanding of God on those theological commitments established in the early, undivided era of the first five centuries of the Church, and have seen no need to add to the doctrines inherited from such times; or to acknowledge that unlike other Reformation traditions, such as Lutherans or Calvinists, we have not tended to identify ourselves with definitive doctrinal statements but instead with the historic Apostles' and Nicene Creeds and with particular patterns of common prayer. These statements are indeed true, but they don't mean that Anglicans have no doctrine. That sentiment has encouraged us to direct disproportionate degrees of scholarly enquiry towards history, so that in a study of Anglicanism it is quite normal for the greater part of the work to be given over to history rather than doctrine. In this book I have tried to set a different course: I *begin* in Chapter 1 with doctrine, in Chapter 2 I look to the sources of doctrine, in Chapter 3 proceed to the ways those doctrines are most visibly manifested and only in Chapter 4 do I come to history, by way of conclusion. Perhaps the most significant Anglican method of perceiving doctrine is the context set in Chapter 3: not abstract, never simply a series of propositions, but always in relation to worship, ministry and mission.

Anglicans are sometimes teased for regarding themselves as particularly well placed to participate in ecumenical dialogue and for being, like Israel, a people through whom others may find a blessing. The teasing is fitting, for it is surely for others to identify traditions that are helpful in catalyzing the reunion of the Churches, rather than for us to award ourselves the accolade. Nonetheless the word 'and' appears close to the heart of the identity described in these pages. The most obvious case of this 'and' lies in the phrase 'Catholic and Reformed'. Not every Anglican agrees with the convergence identified here. But in general the desire – which goes back to Queen Elizabeth I and the settlement of 1559 – that the Church should have a Catholic shape, with bishops, priests and deacons, and sacraments of baptism and Eucharist, while having a Protestant emphasis on the authority of Scripture and the preaching of the Word, remains one of the Anglican Communion's most deeply held commitments. We have no revered founder, no pivotal item of doctrine, no egregious error of another group of Christians against which we are ever to be defined, and no pivotal interpreter through whose definitive interpretation of Scripture all must be evaluated. There was never a crucial time when we have felt we could simply take up the New Testament and begin anew. Instead we have a tradition of common prayer, a general commitment to the well-being of all, including non-members of the Church, and a desire to seek a faith that can be shared by a wide diversity of temperaments and classes of people.

In these pages I make regular reference to three documents. Most often I refer to one or more of the forms of liturgy in use in the Anglican Communion, often known as the Book of Common Prayer, and most recently in England emerging as a series of texts known as *Common Worship*. This is because Anglicans are notable for the way their doctrine and ethics emerge from the crucible of corporate prayer.

I also refer to one doctrinal statement, the Thirty-Nine Articles, as articulated by a convocation of the English Church under Archbishop Matthew Parker in 1563, and as included in the 1662 Book of Common Prayer. While this statement does not have the authority of the historic creeds and is, particularly on matters of salvation and the Church, sometimes unhelpfully preoccupied with the particular quarrels of the sixteenth century, it provides a helpful though not definitive reference point for pursuing a Catholic-and-Reformed approach to doctrine, and that is the spirit in which I quote from it in this book. While I grew up regarding the Thirty-Nine Articles as narrow and dated, and understand that many continue to hold this view, I have come to find it a fruitful conversation partner and a significant though not exhaustive or definitive foundation statement of Anglican belief.

One other document on which I draw is the Chicago-Lambeth Quadrilateral, which arose in the late nineteenth century as a proposal for the reunion of the Roman Catholic and Orthodox Churches around four principles: the Old and New Testaments; the Nicene and Apostles' Creeds; the sacraments of baptism and Eucharist; and the historic episcopate, locally adapted.

By what authority do I claim to be able to speak for a whole branch of the worldwide Church? None. I perhaps aim to speak *with* it and *to* it, more than *for* it. My words, particularly in Chapter 1, are more earnest prescription than neutral observation: I recognize that my account goes beyond simple description. I portray the faith to which I trust all Christians in the Anglican Communion subscribe – but I know the reality is much more diverse than the way I present it. For most of that diversity I give genuine thanks. My attempt to represent the breadth of the Church is to be found not so much in the first three chapters but more in the final one, which is specifically designed to be descriptive. Chapter 4, in short, bears testimony to the complications that arise when trying to live the first three chapters.

One final underlying aim of this book is to assist American and English Anglicans and Episcopalians in understanding one another. The first three chapters outline the way our doctrine is shared. The fourth describes how our respective histories and contexts are different, bringing out contrasts between the established Church of England and the non-established Episcopal Church, and between the varieties of contexts that characterize the Churches of the Anglican Communion. If bonds of affection between our provinces are to be sustained, affirmed, fostered and deepened, members of our Churches need to appreciate, at least in outline, the different pressures, tensions and assumptions and narratives within which we are each working.

And this goal of increasing interecclesial understanding is also a personal one. I was born in the Anglican Church of Canada, raised in the Church of England, trained for ordination in the Scottish Episcopal Church and currently minister, in an interdenominational setting, as a priest of The Episcopal Church in the USA. I have been enriched by the contexts in which I have lived and served. I trust, and pray, that these diverse contexts will long continue to enrich one another.

1 The Faith

Introduction: The Triune God

God is in Christ. This central statement of Christian belief crystallizes a number of distinct but related convictions.

First, the historical figure Jesus of Nazareth, born in Bethlehem, living in Galilee, dying and rising in Jerusalem, embodies everything good, beautiful, and true that comes from the inmost being of God. Jesus is the centripetal goal to which all searches for truth must look, and Jesus is the centrifugal force from which all goodness flows. If one wants to know who God is and what God is like and how God acts, Jesus is the touchstone of any answer.

Second, Christ is not just *from the heart of* God: Christ *is* God. Our notion of God is shaped – or reshaped – in the light of having seen God in Christ. God is the same God who is revealed in the Old Testament and known to the Jews – the one God. But God is also made known in Christ, and that is a different but closely related notion of God, which thenceforth governs all perceptions of God.

Third, it is not just that God *was* in Christ when Jesus was walking around Galilee in the first century. God *is* in Christ today. That not only indicates a conviction that Christ is risen from the dead, but given that Christ returned whence he came, it suggests a third dimension of God that does not have a human body but makes the risen Christ present in people and actions and events of God's choosing. Jesus spoke of God as one with whom he had an intimate, familial, unbreakable bond: he used the language of father and son. But he also spoke of there being a regular, perpetual presence of God among his followers after he had returned to his Father. This presence was one of comfort, counsel and advocacy, whom we call the Holy Spirit.

Thus God came to be known as Father, Son and Holy Spirit. This is a relationship of three 'persons', distinct from one another yet in one 'substance' – sharing one being. They are equal with one another yet each has different roles; but even in these different roles the whole of God is present in each one. The first of the Thirty-Nine Articles states that:

> There is but one living and true God, everlasting, without body, parts, or passions; of infinite power, wisdom, and goodness; the Maker, and Preserver of all things both visible and invisible. And in unity of this Godhead there be three Persons, of one substance, power, and eternity; the Father, the Son, and the Holy Ghost.[1]

Concerns have been raised in recent years that this language is unhelpfully male. It can be (and has been) invoked to affirm patriarchal construals of human relationships. There is no doctrinal justification for associating gender with God. However, Jesus' own usage argues for retaining the traditional vocabulary, and as yet no alternative nomenclature has emerged that retains both the personal and the interdependent dimensions of the Trinity. So this most central element of Christian belief – the name of the triune God – remains, at this time, an unresolved area.

Transformation in Christ

The heart of the Christian faith is that God came among human beings as Jesus of Nazareth. Jesus is God, fully present to humanity, and humanity, fully present to God. Jesus expressed the full possibility of being human, and made known the full

---

1 http://www.churchofengland.org/prayer-worship/worship/book-of-common-prayer/articles-of-religion.aspx.

reality of God. The coming of God in Jesus broke down the dividing wall between God and humanity and the false separations between humans and one another – and indeed the whole creation. This coming is the central moment in history: everything before it was a preparation for it and everything since has taken place in the light of it. This transformation may be perceived in four dimensions.

First, Jesus' incarnation and birth. Jesus 'was made man' (in the words of the Nicene Creed); in the words of John 1.14, 'The Word became flesh and lived among us.' This means Jesus was fully human, fully divine, and yet was one person. The Chalcedonian Creed of 451, which expresses most explicitly the 'hypostatic union' of Jesus' human and divine nature, states that Jesus is:

> to be acknowledged in two natures, inconfusedly, unchangeably, indivisibly, inseparably; the distinction of natures being by no means taken away by the union, but rather the property of each nature being preserved, and concurring in one Person and one Subsistence, not parted or divided into two persons, but one and the same Son.[2]

In other words, Jesus was and is a single person – but in that single person lies both a divine and a human nature, which are not blended but remain distinct.

One important way in which this conviction is expressed is in the doctrine of the virgin birth, which maintains that Jesus was born of a union between the Virgin Mary and the Holy Spirit, and that neither Joseph nor any other man was involved in Jesus' conception. Hence the Chalcedonian Creed states that Jesus was 'begotten before all ages of the Father according to the Godhead, and in these latter days, for us and for our salvation, born of the Virgin Mary, the Mother of God, according to the Manhood'. This doctrine emphasizes that salvation is entirely God's initiative. The term for 'birth' in the original Greek of Matthew 1.18 is 'genesis'. This hints that the con-

---

2 http://www.creeds.net/ancient/chalcedon.htm.

ception of Jesus – not specifically in Mary's womb, but God's decision never to be except to be for and with us in Christ – is the beginning of all creation, of all life, of all salvation, of everything that matters. Thus the creation itself was a kind of virgin birth because it was creation from nothing, and it was brought about by the Holy Spirit. And the virgin birth was a new creation, or perhaps even the original creation because it too was brought about in some ways out of nothing, by the action of the Holy Spirit.[3]

Another dimension of the belief in God's enfleshment in Christ is the delicate balance between the ways Jesus Christ is like humanity and the ways he is not. The Chalcedonian Creed states simply that Christ is 'in all things like unto us, without sin'. The second of the Thirty-Nine Articles adds, however, an extra assertion: that Jesus *truly suffered*. The Nicene Creed makes a similar claim when it recalls that Jesus 'suffered under Pontius Pilate'. If Jesus is to be regarded as fully God, he cannot sin, for God is 'perfect in power, in love and purity', as the hymn puts it.[4] But if Jesus is to be regarded as fully human, he must suffer. The notion, known as Docetism, that Jesus only appeared to be human and therefore could not experience human suffering, and thus only *seemed* to suffer on the cross, is a distortion of Christian doctrine that theologians have long sought to eradicate. Showing how Jesus entered wholly into human experience, yet without sin, and exploring how Jesus suffered, but in a way that expressed, rather than took away from the perfection of God, have been two projects close to the heart of Christology since the beginning.

As we shall see in Chapter 4, Jesus' incarnation has been a particular emphasis of Anglican theology, particularly in the nineteenth and twentieth centuries.

Second, Jesus' ministry in Galilee. Despite constituting the majority of the narrative in all four Gospels, this has never

---

3 For a more developed account of this argument see Samuel Wells, *Speaking the Truth: Preaching in a Pluralistic Culture* (Nashville: Abingdon, 2008), pp. 52–8.

4 Reginald Heber, 'Holy, Holy, Holy, Lord God Almighty'.

become the subject of controversy in the way other aspects of Jesus' life have. Thus, for example, the Nicene Creed omits it altogether; and the Thirty-Nine Articles make no mention of it either – it is not even to be found in Article XXXV among the list of subjects of approved homilies. Yet such silence reflects consensus rather than neglect.

After Jesus was baptized by John and commissioned by the voice of the Father and the descent of the Holy Spirit, he faced a time of testing and temptation. Then he emerged to proclaim the reign of God and call disciples. The number of disciples – twelve, the same number as the tribes of Israel – reflected the way Jesus was reconstituting the people of God. This was also expressed in his ministry of teaching, in which, like Moses, he gave the people a way to live faithfully under God; and in his performance of miracles, enacted parables in which, like Elijah and Elisha, he showed his oneness with God and his sovereignty over the human body and the forces that oppress it, such as sickness, hunger and mighty storm. He also attracted controversy, and in his disputes with the religious and social authorities of his time forthrightly proclaimed the righteousness of God that transcended their limited and self-serving percep-tions. Thus Jesus *declared* the present and coming reign of God in his teaching, *demonstrated* it in his miracles and *demanded* a response by calling people to follow him.

Third, Jesus' passion and death. The Gospels record that, during his ministry in Galilee, Jesus turned towards Jerusalem, anticipating that his arrival there would presage his violent death. His challenge to the religious and social authorities of his day – demonstrated beyond question in his cleansing of the temple and either implicit or explicit in his teaching and heal-ing – provoked a plot to have him executed by the Romans. The crowds that had applauded his entrance into Jerusalem on a donkey turned against him days later and called for him to be crucified. Jesus died one of the most agonizing deaths imaginable – slowly asphyxiated while suspended by nails driven through his hands, all the while mocked and reviled by his persecutors and deserted by most of his disciples.

The death of Jesus is the focal moment of Christian devotion, in a way that transcends the precise historical circumstances that surround it. The crucifixion, it seems, is what happens when the profound and utter goodness of God comes face to face with the fickle and faithless machinations of humankind. The tremors resulting from the first tree, of Adam in the Garden of Eden, finally emerge in the second tree, of Jesus on Calvary. But somehow the horror of the cross lies deep in the purpose of God – hence the day of its commemoration is known as *Good* Friday. This goodness is traceable in two further Old Testament passages. One is the binding of Isaac in Genesis 22 – where Abraham is called to give up his only son and yet is delivered when God sees his obedience and tells him to offer a ram instead. Jesus is seen as both the obedient son and the sacrificial ram, who dies in the place of others. The other passage is the servant songs of Isaiah 40–55 (Israel comes to see its vocation as suffering in order to reconcile God to the world, especially Isaiah 53), where the language of being 'led like a lamb to the slaughter' quickly became identified with Jesus' journey to the cross.

On a simply human level Jesus did not *need* to go to the cross – he was an innocent man and he could have found plenty of ways of avoiding the attentions of those who meant him harm. He made a free choice, just as hearers of his story ever since have made a free choice whether or not to recognize his suffering as God's gift to them. The poignancy of this free choice is most visible in his tortured prayer in the Garden of Gethsemane where he says, 'My Father, if it is possible, let this cup pass from me; yet not what I want but what you want' (Matt. 26.39). His violent death was nonetheless almost inevitable, since on a spiritual level humanity seems incapable of tolerating profound goodness for very long, and on a practical level Jesus seems to have been unwilling or unable to cease his public ministry, which made him a perpetual source of exasperation to the authorities. Among many features of Jesus' suffering and death the following have attracted particular attention:

- *Jesus' vicarious suffering as a sacrifice.* It is hinted at in the Gospels (the term 'ransom' in Mark 10.45 for example) and made much more explicit in Paul's letters that Jesus died for the sake of sinners – whether Israel or all whom God has chosen or all people or all creation. Here lies the significance of Jesus' death coinciding with Passover, since the blood of the lamb signalled the angel of the Lord to pass over the houses of the Israelites in Exodus, and here the blood of Jesus, the Lamb of God, accordingly causes God to pass over the people's sins. It is not clear precisely why Jesus' death causes God to 'pass over' human sin, but the echo of the Passover lamb is frequently evident in the New Testament.

- *Jesus' non-resistance and forgiving demeanour as he went to his death.* The words, 'He saved others; he cannot save himself' (Mark 15.31) and 'Father, forgive them; for they do not know what they are doing' (Luke 23.34) perfectly express the irony and the pathos of Jesus' defenceless death. Jesus, in an extreme working-out of the logic of the incarnation, was handed over into the mercy of the merciless. Having started his life with his arms bound by a loving mother in swaddling clothes, he ended it with his arms nailed down by enemies on a cross: but still he loved his enemies as much as he loved his mother.

- *The isolation of Jesus, not just among human beings but even perhaps in the heart of God.* Jesus' words from the cross, 'My God, my God, why have you forsaken me?' (Mark 15.34), have sometimes been interpreted as expressing the profound alienation of Jesus, even within the eternal and unbreakable mutual indwelling of the Holy Trinity. Whether this truly means there was a cross in the heart of God from the foundation of the world, or whether this is a grief and sorrow Jesus bore on behalf of sinners for a precise period of time, is not an easy question to resolve. (It could also be that since Jesus is quoting Psalm 22, which ends positively, the words are actually a coded declaration of hope.) Regardless of the exact import of the words, they are a searing challenge to recognize the depth of human alienation from God, the extent of Jesus' identification with the human predicament and the limitlessness of God's commitment to redeeming the world, even to the point of letting this alienation penetrate God's inner being.

The Thirty-Nine Articles insist that 'As Christ died for us, and was buried, so also is it to be believed, that he went down into Hell' (Article III). This is noted in some versions of the Apostles' Creed in the words, 'He descended into hell' (other versions say 'He descended to the dead'); but it is not mentioned in the Nicene Creed. The scriptural witness for this doctrine is slight, but the point is chiefly to address the complex issue of the salvation of those who had died before the coming of Christ. This suggestion, that Christ 'harrowed' hell, a tradition in many places recalled in the liturgy of Holy Saturday, is a gesture towards resolving the anomalies that arise when salvation is restricted to those who believe, including the eternal status of those who for a host of reasons never had the chance to hear the gospel.

Fourth, Jesus' resurrection and ascension. The resurrection of the incarnate Lord, Jesus Christ, is the focus of Christian faith, the historic beginning of Christian worship and the foundation of Christian hope. This is because it represents – or achieves – God's sovereignty over sin and death and shows that the conflict embodied on the cross is resolved forever. In the resurrection of Jesus, Christians see the promise of their own resurrection and the restoration of all creation.

A number of factors make the resurrection a complex doctrine. The Gospel accounts do not narrate the resurrection itself in the way that they narrate Jesus' crucifixion and death, for example. They simply describe Jesus' appearances to Mary and the disciples. The precise moment and manner of the resurrection remains veiled as a mystery. Meanwhile Jesus' resurrection appears to be a unique and unprecedented historical event, suspending conventional laws of nature and almost defying description. While Jesus is recorded as raising Lazarus (John 11.1–44) and the widow's son at Nain (Luke 7.11–15), his own resurrection is different because his bodily form, while still bearing the marks of the nails (John 20.25–27), is capable of sudden inexplicable appearances and disappearances (Luke 24.31, 36). Some believers, while wishing to affirm God's sovereignty over sin and death, have found the notion of such a unique, bodily resurrection hard to endorse. It has been quite common in such circles to make a distinction between spiritual and bodily resurrection, with an approving nod to the former.

The Thirty-Nine Articles are unequivocal in their affirmation of Jesus' physical resurrection: 'Christ did truly rise again from death, and took again his body, with flesh, bones, and all things appertaining to the perfection of Man's nature' (Article IV). This is not just a recognition of scriptural authority, for it indicates three further things. First, God's sovereignty over sin and death and his offer of forgiveness and everlasting life is the central point at stake, and every effort should be made to preserve faith in that sovereignty, rather than be waylaid by convictions about the physical universe. Second, it is vital that the resurrection demonstrates the completion of Christ's work on the cross. However precise the Church's understanding of what was achieved on the cross, the resurrection is not simply an affirmation of it but an integral part and completion of it. Third, the tendency to downplay the human body and to assert the primacy of the soul is a deep-seated strand in Christian theology and piety, going back to the Neoplatonic philosophy fashionable in the early centuries of the Church; but it contrasts with the very physical statement of faith that focuses on the incarnation of God in Christ. The logical implication of a non-physical resurrection for Christ is, almost inevitably, the anticipation of a non-physical hope of resurrection for Christians. The relationship between the resurrection of Jesus Christ and the resurrection of all believers – or perhaps all people, or all things – is not a simple one. Without doubt the resurrection of Jesus completes the work of the cross in restoring to the believer – through the forgiveness of sins – everything that has been lost in the past and – through the offer of everlasting life – everything that one might fear to lose in the future. The risen body of Jesus, bearing the marks of his passion yet with unprecedented powers, aptly portrays this double gift. But it gives no precise clue about what *form* the believer's risen body may take nor *where* it may reappear (not in this life, like Jesus) nor *when* it may appear. Some have taken their cue from Jesus' words to the thief on the cross, 'today you will be with me in Paradise' (Luke 23.43) and taken them to indicate an immediate entry into heaven on the death of the believer. Others have taken the frequent references to 'the last day' to indicate a general judgement for all creation, or all people, before which those who have died will remain in an unresolved state. Others again have taken the words of Revelation 21 to be normative and have perceived God to be preparing a new heaven and a new earth that will transform all known forms of life largely beyond recognition, thus rendering hopes for merely individual survival secondary.

The key point about Jesus' ascension into heaven is not to speculate about whether heaven is 'up there' and thus whether or not Jesus truly 'went up'. It is rather that Jesus had completed his work among us. This is a point of struggle for many Christians, who may be inclined to feel, looking at the woes of the world, that there is a great deal left for him still to do. But it is essential to the faith to hold on to the conviction that Jesus has opened up the past through the forgiveness of sins and opened the future through the gift of eternal life, and any addition would be less, not more. The sending of the Holy Spirit and the final consummation on the last day are the logical fulfilment of Christ's coming, but they must not be described in such a way that might suggest Jesus' work in itself was anything less than complete. One negative consequence of losing a conviction that Christ's work is complete is gaining a false notion that we must complete it ourselves: our work must truly continue the trajectory of Christ's work, but any idea that we ourselves can save the world is bad for us and bad for the world, besides running contrary to the evidence of fragile and flawed human history.[5]

---

5 This is clearly not the last word on mission. For further reflection see Chapter 3.

The People of God

Jesus was a Jew. Christians have repeatedly denied or at least overlooked this fact through the centuries. This deliberate or unintended ignorance has persisted despite the fact that the New Testament explores Jesus' Jewishness at length, particularly in Matthew's Gospel, where Jesus is presented as the new Moses. The Church's treatment of the Jews, particularly in its second millennium, constitutes one of its greatest failures. To understand Jesus one first needs to speak of Israel. There are four aspects of the term 'Israel' that together play a significant role in providing a context and backdrop to the Christian faith.

First, Israel and covenant. Israel names the people to whom the character and purposes of God are disclosed and through whom all the peoples of the earth are to find a blessing. The early chapters of Genesis tell of two paths God might have taken. One is to work with and through all humanity – represented by Adam and Eve. The other is to settle upon one righteous person – represented by Noah. Instead God chose one people, beginning with Abraham; and the rest of Genesis shows how that people's identity emerges not through their own merit but through the grace of God. After Noah God promised never again to destroy the earth (Gen. 9.11). This then becomes the dynamic that animates the whole Bible: how God will redeem humankind through a particular people without destroying the earth and in a way that blesses all peoples. The defining experience of Israel lies in the exodus. The exodus, largely narrated in the book of the same name in the Bible and the three that follow it, refers to Israel's time of slavery in Egypt, the simultaneous disclosure to Moses in the burning bush of both the identity of God and God's purpose to liberate the people, Israel's deliverance through God's miraculous hand, the giving of the covenant to Moses on Mount Sinai and the entry into and conquest of the Promised Land under Joshua after 40 years in the wilderness. This sequence of events became the touchstone for Israel's identity and the standard of Israel's faithfulness. For example, the prophets saw the oppression of landless and powerless people during the time of the kings and interpreted such injustice as a forgetfulness of who Israel truly was: for God had visited Israel when Israel was in desperate straits, and Israel should show understanding and gratitude by treating the poor the way God had treated Israel.

The term that gathers together all these dimensions of Israel's experience is covenant. Covenant also expresses the way various nations in Christian history have identified God's blessing to Israel and assigned it to themselves. Examples include the English in the nineteenth century, the Afrikaners in the twentieth century and some dimensions of the United States today, among each of which influential spokespersons have seen themselves as God's chosen people with a special mission.[6]

The second key element of Israel in the Christian faith is Israel's relationship to Jesus. God laments that the Sinai covenant has been broken but resolves to remain Israel's parent (Hos. 11.1–11), and promises that there will be a new covenant, written on the hearts of the people (Jer. 31.31–35). Early Christians quickly identified that covenant with the one of which Jesus spoke at the Last Supper (Mark 14.24; Matt. 26.28; Luke 22.20), and perceived the blood of Jesus as sealing the covenant, just as the blood of the lamb ensured the angel of the Lord passed over the houses of the Hebrews on the eve of the exodus (Exod. 12.13, 23). Jesus' ministry includes many gestures that imitate and revive dimensions of Israel's story. He calls 12 disciples (Matt. 10.1–4; Mark 3.16–19; Luke 6.14–16), recalling the 12 tribes of Israel; he is baptized at the Jordan (Matt. 3.13–17; Mark 1.9–11; Luke 3.21–22; John 1.31–34), where

---

6 The theologian Oliver O'Donovan offers another way to appreciate Israel's heritage faithfully. He speaks of God's reign, which brings together the decisive action of God in securing Israel's victory over enemies and in offering salvation. He next speaks of God's law, as the covenant made with Israel on Mount Sinai and the ordering of life and exercise of judgement that it entailed. He then speaks of God's land, referring to the Promised Land as the visible token of God's provision. Finally he points to the people's response in praise. Oliver O'Donovan, *The Desire of the Nations: Rediscovering the Roots of Political Theology* (Cambridge: Cambridge University Press, 1996 [repr. 2002]), pp. 30–49.

Israel came into the land (Deut. 9.1); he goes up on a mount like Moses (Exod. 19.20; Matt. 5.1) to explain a code of ethics that improvises on the Sinai covenant (Matt. 5–7); he heals like Elijah (1 Kings 17.17–24; Luke 7.11–15); goes down to Egypt (Matt. 2.13–15) like his forebears did (Gen. 47.27); and so on. All the hopes of Israel converge on the person of Jesus.

Yet Christians continue to read not just the story of Jesus in the New Testament but also the story of Israel in the Old, and continue to call both testaments their Bible. The place of the Old Testament is thus the third dimension of Israel's place in the Christian imagination. Caricatures of the Old Testament persist. They include the view that the God of the Old Testament is a warrior, unlike the peaceable God of the New; that the Old Testament's usefulness resides simply in its prophecies of the coming Messiah; and that the Old Testament is full of ritual and prohibition whereas the New is full of grace and freedom. By contrast the Thirty-Nine Articles insist that the Old Testament is an indispensable part of the Bible and that 'both in the Old and New Testament everlasting life is offered to Mankind by Christ' (Article VII) – in other words, that the gospel is to be discerned in the Old as well as in the New Testament. However, the articles also maintain a longstanding tradition first described in detail in the thirteenth century by Alexander of Hales and other Franciscan theologians and adopted by Thomas Aquinas, that a distinction may be made between the ritual/ceremonial, the civil and the moral commandments.[7] The moral commandments remain binding even though with the new covenant the other commandments have ceased to be so (Article VII). Another subtle distinction concerns the place of the Apocrypha. The Articles include First and Second Esdras among the canonical books and list a further 14 books as ones to be read 'for example of life and instruction of manners', but not as sources or grounds of doctrine (Article VI).

---

7 The threefold division had been anticipated by the Jewish philosopher Maimonides. See Matthew Levering, *Christ's Fulfilment of Torah and Temple: Salvation according to Thomas Aquinas* (Notre Dame, IN: University of Notre Dame Press, 2002), pp. 6–8.

But what then of the Jews? This is the fourth aspect of the place of Israel in relation to Christianity. From the early centuries of the Church, Christians have had a tendency to forget that Jesus was born of a Jewish mother and that the first disciples were Jews; to speak as if all Jews bear responsibility for killing Jesus, highlighting the Gospels' accounts of the raging mob (Mark 15.13–14; Matt. 27.22–25; Luke 23.18–23) rather than the first-century Jewish and Roman administrations in Jerusalem in particular; and to misunderstand, misrepresent or even demonize post-biblical Judaism. The history of Christian relations with Judaism has been largely made up of Christian inability to deal with Jewish difference, and a catalogue of prejudices and misappropriated scriptural texts, sometimes exacerbated and manipulated for political advantage, frequently issuing in violent persecution, evolving in the nineteenth century into explicit anti-Semitism and culminating in the Nazi Holocaust.

While there is widespread and almost universal repentance in the Anglican Communion today about this shameful history, the precise place of the Jews in the Christian view of the world and the Church is still unclear. There is no consensus on whether Christians should, for example, still seek the conversion of Jews to Christianity. It is not clear what is the status of God's promises to the Jews: while they still have a special and unshakeable place in God's heart, the incorporation of the Gentiles into God's people has clearly altered that relationship – but exactly how and to what extent is not certain. It seems these things are for God to know and for the Church to discover. It is not at all clear what should be the understanding of the secular contemporary State of Israel, to what degree the State of Israel should be associated with the identity and destiny of the Jewish people, and what are the rights and responsibilities of the State of Israel in relation to its non-Jewish inhabitants and neighbours.

The Holy Spirit and the Church

How does the salvation offered in Christ take shape for human beings in history – most notably, for believers today? The answer to that question is, the Holy Spirit. Article V of the Thirty-Nine Articles states that 'The Holy Ghost, proceeding from the Father and the Son, is of one substance, majesty, and glory, with the Father and the Son, very and eternal God.' This affirms that the Holy Spirit is an equal member of the Trinity and thus fully God, but it remains reticent on the actual work of the Holy Spirit – a tendency in Anglican theology ever since. But the words of the Nicene Creed encourage further articulation: 'I believe in the Holy Ghost, the Lord and Giver of Life; who proceeds from the Father and the Son; who with the Father and the Son together is worshipped and glorified; who spoke by the prophets.' The sixth-century addition of the words 'and the Son' is strongly disputed by the Eastern Orthodox Churches. The Anglican tradition has sided with the Western Church, maintaining that only if the Spirit is understood as proceeding from both Father and Son is it possible to insist that all activities of the Spirit must resemble the God made known in Jesus. And that is the key to recognizing the work of the Spirit: it makes people and organizations and activities look like Jesus.

What the Holy Spirit does is to overcome the distance of space and time between Christ and the believer and make Jesus present to the Church today. For example, the risen and ascended Jesus sits at the right hand of the Father but the Holy Spirit makes Jesus present in the elements of bread and wine in the service of Holy Communion. The Holy Spirit is also the giver of life: from hovering over the waters (Gen. 1.2) to giving the believer new birth (John 3.3–8) to healing the divisions of Babel portrayed in the tongues of fire on the day of Pentecost (Acts 2.1–4). This new life is fundamentally one that sets people free – as Jesus proclaims in the synagogue in Nazareth, 'The Spirit of the Lord is upon me, because he has anointed me to bring good news to the poor. He has sent me to proclaim release to the captives and recovery of sight to the blind, to let the oppressed go free, to proclaim the year of the Lord's favour' (Luke 4.18–19). All of these works of the Spirit concern release from bondage. And the Spirit stands alongside believers as they withstand trials and temptations: Jesus says, 'I will ask the Father, and he will give you another Advocate, to be with you forever. This is the Spirit of truth . . . When the Advocate comes, whom I will send to you from the Father, the Spirit of truth who comes from the Father, he will testify on my behalf' (John 14.16; 15.26). And this will be at the most challenging times: 'When they bring you to trial and hand you over, do not worry beforehand about what you are to say; but say whatever is given you at that time, for it is not you who speak, but the Holy Spirit' (Mark 13.11). In the rite of baptism in the Church of England, the Holy Spirit is named no fewer than five times in the prayer of thanksgiving over the water. The prayer describes many of the roles of the Spirit.

> We thank you, Almighty God, for the gift of water to sustain, refresh and cleanse all life. Over water the Holy Spirit moved in the beginning of creation . . . In water your Son Jesus received the baptism of John and was anointed by the Holy Spirit as the Messiah . . . We thank you, Father, for the water of baptism . . . Through it we are reborn by the Holy Spirit . . . Now sanctify this water that, by the power of your Holy Spirit, they may be cleansed from sin and born again . . . Renewed in your image, may they . . . continue for ever in the risen life of Jesus Christ our Lord; to whom with you and the Holy Spirit be all honour and glory, now and for ever.[8]

But the Spirit is not just addressed to individuals. The Church is that body of people in whom the Holy Spirit corporately dwells. The Spirit brings unity to that body. Just as the Spirit communicates the bondedness of the Trinity, so the Spirit

---

8 The Church of England, *Common Worship: Initiation Services* (London: Church House Publishing 1998), pp. 23–4.

draws together diverse communities and overcomes dividing walls of hostility. To do this the Spirit gives the Church gifts. The purpose of these gifts, as Paul repeatedly stresses, is the upbuilding of the body as a whole.

> To each is given the manifestation of the Spirit for the common good. To one is given through the Spirit the utterance of wisdom, and to another the utterance of knowledge according to the same Spirit, to another faith by the same Spirit, to another gifts of healing by the one Spirit, to another the working of miracles, to another prophecy, to another the discernment of spirits, to another various kinds of tongues, to another the interpretation of tongues. All these are activated by one and the same Spirit, who allots to each one individually just as the Spirit chooses. (1 Cor. 12.7–11)

The emphasis in Anglicanism has generally been that the more dramatic gifts, such as speaking in tongues, are to take their place in the background, with the more abiding gifts such as faith, hope and love in the foreground (1 Cor. 13.1–3, 13). A community receiving the gifts of the Spirit in appropriately upbuilding ways may be expected to exhibit the fruits of the Spirit: 'love, joy, peace, patience, kindness, generosity, faithfulness, gentleness, and self-control' (Gal. 5.22–23).

Part of the role of such gifts is to point the Church's attention towards the climax of God's story in the eschaton, the 'last day'. The Spirit is described variously as a seal, down-payment or guarantee of God's promises. For example, the Ephesians are told that they 'were marked with the seal of the promised Holy Spirit; this is the pledge of our inheritance towards redemption as God's own people' (Eph. 1.13–14). One way this is expressed in worship is in the conclusion of the Great Thanksgiving prayer at the Eucharist. This third part of the prayer often dwells on the way the empowerment of the Spirit leads Christians to seek the Lord's consummation in actions advancing justice and peace, and to see the Spirit especially revealed among the oppressed of the earth – often, and increasingly, in

17

reference to the damaged soil, seas and skies themselves. The Thirty-Nine Articles describe the visible Church as a congregation of the faithful 'in which the pure Word of God is preached, and the Sacraments . . . duly ministered according to Christ's ordinance' (Article XIX). The Church and the Spirit are vitally interlinked because it is above all the Church that makes visible the possibilities of human interaction released by the saving work of Christ. Thus the Church is the primary – though by no means the only – sphere of the Spirit's activity. But if the Church is to be and to be seen as both human and divine, like Christ, and not just a mundane and self-serving club or bureaucracy, the Spirit must infuse the structures of its life in personal, liberating, life-giving and unifying ways.

The Nicene Creed describes the Church as 'one, holy, catholic, and apostolic'. Each of these words deserves attention and highlights the work of the Spirit. The word 'one' refers to the Church's unity, which has always been a central concern of Anglican Churches. Often they describe themselves as both Catholic and Reformed. Sometimes, for example during the nineteenth-century Catholic revival in the Church of England, they perceive themselves as offering a *via media* between Rome and Geneva (or even Rome and Constantinople). In these ways Anglicans highlight their role – perhaps their calling – as agents of unity not just among diverse Christians in a single territory but among Christians throughout the world. Jesus' words in his farewell discourses resonate strongly with Anglicans:

'I ask not only on behalf of these, but also on behalf of those who will believe in me through their word, that they may all be one. As you, Father, are in me and I am in you, may they also be in us, so that the world may believe that you have sent me. The glory that you have given me I have given them, so that they may be one, as we are one, I in them and you in me, that they may become completely one, so that the world may know that you have sent me and have loved them even as you have loved me.' (John 17.20–23)

Here we see that unity is both about reflecting the glory of God and about representing God to the unbelieving 'world'. These two concerns motivate Anglicans in their desire not only to preserve the unity of their own communion but to see their communion as having a special vocation to draw together the stray sheep of the world's disparate communions. The Church is not simply a means to an end; it is not simply a boat from which to fish for new disciples or a platform from which to organize for social justice. It is called to embody in its own life the redemption that it preaches and the unity-in-diversity it beholds in the triune God. Thus splits in the body are especially damaging for Anglicans because their communion is precisely intended to express and embrace the full diversity of the body of Christ. This is the significance of the words, 'He is our peace; in his flesh he has made both groups into one and has broken down the dividing wall, that is, the hostility between us' (Eph. 2.14). Thus the failure of Christians in the Anglican Communion to remain one body offers a damaging prima facie argument that the dividing wall has not been broken down and the gospel is not true.

The word 'holy' looks in a different direction. It points to the sanctifying work of the Spirit in making Christians more like God from the inside out. For some Christian traditions this has led to an emphasis on visible holiness; in the contemporary idiom, 'If you were accused of being a Christian, would there be enough evidence to convict you?' While there are significant strands of seeking personal sanctification in Anglicanism (particularly in England in the sixteenth and seventeenth centuries and in the movement that became Methodism in the eighteenth century), the overall tendency has been to perceive holiness in devotional rather than visible and ethical terms. In other words, holiness has been less about being set apart and more about simply being forgiven. Each regular act of worship – morning and evening prayer and holy communion – includes an expectation of some kind of formal confessing of sins and receiving of absolution; this demonstrates how central repentance and forgiveness are to notions of worship among Anglicans. There

is a profound dimension of personal spirituality in the Anglican tradition, but this is less about being set apart and more
about attaining a rhythm of life in accord with the rhythm of
the saints. Meanwhile, particularly in the industrial era, there
is a significant tradition of social holiness, attending to the suffering of the many and the welfare of all; but again this is less
about being the 'light of the world', a people distinct and apart,
and more about being 'the salt of the earth', an incarnational
presence in and among.

'Catholic' (which literally means universal) asks whether the
Church is as gloriously diverse as God's world. For Anglicans,
'catholic' is not a noun identifying an individual member of a
particular Church but an adjective that points to the wideness
of God's mercy. The key to the Anglican vision is the claim
that the Church can be one and catholic at the same time –
that it can contain and embrace all God's people and yet at
the same time remain coherent and at peace with itself. Here
there are seeds of a significant tension between the vision of the
Church of England and Anglican expressions in the rest of the
Communion. The Church of England in general understands
its vocation as existing for all people residing in England,
whether Anglicans, Christians of other denominations, people
of other faiths or those of no expressed faith. Episcopalian and
Anglican expressions in the rest of the world tend to run on a
tighter membership system, with a disposition towards mission
to, partnership with and dialogue among those beyond that
membership but with the danger that the emphasis is on the
membership itself. For many centuries the heart of the Church
of England's claim to catholicity is that it genuinely is the
catholic Church in England, factually or at the very least prag-
matically and operationally, because it alone exists for all the
people of the land whatever their faith or practice. The Roman
Catholic Church, on the other hand, is not in the fullest sense
catholic because it exists only for those who call themselves
Roman Catholics, a mere 'denomination' (at least in England
if not elsewhere) rather than the Church in the broad, true,
catholic sense of the term. But the very same logic that asserts

the catholicity of the Church of England identifies the inconsistency of that logic when applied to Churches of the broader Anglican Communion. Indeed the very fact that the Church of England has supported and in some cases founded Anglican Churches in parts of the world where Roman Catholicism was already alive and well, runs counter to the claim that the Church of England is the true catholic Church.

Churches in the Anglican Communion outside England have found different ways of expressing their catholicity. They arguably have to work harder to avoid becoming gatherings of the like-minded, and instead seek to be servants of God's diverse creation. But they share the opportunity and vocation to be Churches that seek to reconcile the polarities of Protestant and Catholic, conservative and liberal, personal and political, and include within themselves a diversity little known elsewhere.

Finally, the term 'apostolic' asks the question, 'Would the first apostles recognize us?' Those who have been concerned to claim the full catholicity of the Church of England have insisted that because the bishops became willing partners in Queen Elizabeth I's realignment of the English Church during the Reformation, the apostolic succession of the laying-on of hands going all the way back to Peter (Matt. 16.16–19) was maintained and the Church of England truly remains not only catholic but apostolic. But this is not the only sense in which 'apostolic' has been understood. Apostolic means remaining faithful to the simplicity and sacrifice of the first disciples and to their teaching and fellowship. In this sense the flourishing of many monastic orders, particularly the Franciscans, who model their lives on the example of the poverty of Christ, keeps the Church's apostolicity alive.[9] Anglican scholarship, particularly since the Oxford Movement in the Church of England in the 1830s and beyond, has taken a close interest in the early theologians of the Church, such as Irenaeus of Lyons (died c.202), Athanasius of Alexandria (c.293–373) and Augustine of Hippo (354–430), and this too preserves an apostolic desire to stay

---

9 There were 2,154 celibate Religious in the Anglican Communion in 2009. See *Anglican Religious Life 2010–11* (Norwich: Canterbury Press, 2009), p. 24.

close to the faith of the early Church. Finally the term 'apostle' means one who is sent out as a messenger or ambassador, and this means that the Church, to be apostolic, must constantly set its face to the world in evangelistic and humanitarian mission, sharing and embodying the faith in humble acts of witness and charity. It is, finally, mission that keeps the Church apostolic.

Creation and the Kingdom

Creation does not play a large role in the Thirty-Nine Articles: the triune God is simply referred to as the 'Maker and Preserver of all things both visible and invisible' (Article I), largely honouring the language of the first article of the Nicene Creed – 'Maker of heaven and earth, and of all things visible and invisible'. The fact that creation has not been an especially controversial dimension of theology among Anglicans does not diminish its significance. This may be identified in a number of themes.

Most significantly of all, God was already Trinity – Father, Son and Holy Spirit – before the creation of the universe. This means three related things. First, the Trinity shaped its life to be in relationship with humankind (in Jesus) before there were human beings, indeed a world, indeed a universe, with which to be in relationship. Second, God and the universe are utterly separate from one another; the universe is not made out of God but is made by God out of nothing. God is not in any sense dependent on the universe but the universe is completely dependent on God. Third, the character of God is displayed in relationship with the universe. That relationship is entirely one of God's initiating; the making, befriending and saving of humankind all comes from the overflowing grace of God and is not a necessary, inherent or automatic dimension of creation. This is the meaning of the term 'creation out of nothing': creation had no necessity, it was entirely an act of God's grace. God's will to be in relationship becomes the logic of the universe – but that logic is inherent in God, not in the universe.

Such logic is consistent with the full revelation of God made in Jesus Christ: that is to say, just as the love of God in the coming of Christ is one that is poured out in suffering and at great cost to God, similarly the love of God in creation is poured out in the focusing of God's unlimited freedom on the particular realities of the universe. God gives something up in order wholly to love the creation.

Because the creation is the gift of God it is good. The life that exists within the created order is limited in various ways: its power is finite, its extent is bounded, its flourishing is fragile, its mortality is unavoidable; but nonetheless it is good. The created order is good not just to the extent that human beings can employ it for food, shelter, warmth, clothing or company; it is good for its own sake, whether it relates to human flourishing or not. It is good not just to the extent that it is alive, beautiful or safe; it is good because God created it. But while it is good it is not flawless; perfect flourishing is not an aspect of human – or any animal – experience in creation, and suffering sometimes results from geological, meteorological or countless other characteristics of the created order. Yet while that suffering may render the creation less than perfect it does not thereby render it less than good. Because the creation is good there is no place for any fear that the material world is somehow less than the spiritual, that the earth or the body are temporary devices that will be tossed away when fulfilment comes or that there is some kind of cosmic battle between good and evil whose outcome remains in the balance. St Paul's proclamation of the resurrection of the body (1 Cor. 15.12–28) and the appearance of the new heaven *and the new earth* at the climax of the book of Revelation (Rev. 21.1) affirm God's abiding purpose for the material quality of the creation; when evil is one day not simply defeated but utterly cast out, it will not be at the expense of the physical but its fulfilment.

The creation is an ordered pattern of reflexive relationship, of beings with one another and with God. Thus the term 'nature' is inadequate in two senses. On the one hand, to understand any one creature is not simply to discover its 'nature' (its innate qualities) but to see how it coexists with other creatures and its wider environment. Creatures cannot be understood in isolation. On the other hand, 'nature' as a whole is not free-standing; it is not a contained system. It exists in relationship with God – indeed, as we have seen, it is the 'nature' of God to be so shaped as to be in relationship with the universe. So to say 'creation' is not primarily to make a claim or specula-tion about the origin of the universe but more significantly to underline that there is no being without God – no sphere of independent existence that operates outside relationship to the Holy Trinity.

This is the heart of Anglican responses to questions of the beginnings of the universe and the evolution of humankind. The point is not to read the scriptural accounts (notably Gen-esis 1—2) as a historical/scientific description, it is to see that the triune God is the epitome of relationship and that God's relationship to the world (and the significance of that relation-ship to both God and the world) is displayed in Jesus Christ. There may indeed be evolving patterns of 'natural selection' but each creature finds its purpose not in survival but in its destiny in relationship to Christ. There may indeed have been a Big Bang that set the universe in motion but the key question is not where the world is coming from but where it is going; and the answer lies in the fulfilment of relationship with God.

This notion of creation as inherent, ordered relationship is also the heart of Anglican understandings of ecological con-cerns. The issue is not that God's purposes might be brought to an untimely end should climate change and species deple-tion continue unabated, it is that creation has always been and continues to be fundamentally about mutual interdependence of creatures and their shared environment within the context of relationship with God. Perverting or jeopardizing this coexist-ence is a profound form of disorder even without the eventual harm to the human species itself.

The themes of creation and kingdom are linked not only because they form the beginning and end of the Christian story but because they encompass the breadth of God's activity and purpose beyond the revelation of Scripture and the particular witness of Israel and Church. The kingdom (or reign) of God refers both to the final unfolding of God's purposes at the end of time and to the anticipatory signs of that unfolding that appeared definitively in Jesus but also continue to appear in the work of the Holy Spirit. These signs are the action of God, but human beings can seek to align themselves with God's action by imitating God's ways in such a manner that they too can perform Spirit-filled anticipatory signs of the kingdom.

Anglican theologians have tended to distance themselves from wholly other-worldly and from wholly this-worldly notions of the kingdom of God. Because this world is good and because God will always have a purpose for it, there is no place for a dispensationalist account of the kingdom that foresees precise fulfilment of scriptural texts concerning the number of the elect, their rapture from the earth and the detailed assortment of signs that precede such an apocalyptic future. Because of the abiding character of sin, neither is there a place for a notion of gradual progress that foresees human beings growing nearer to God through moral and social enhancement. The world, while it undoubtedly changes significantly as a result of human endeavour, is not fundamentally better or worse than it was a hundred years ago or will be a hundred years from now. Human endeavour is faithful; but fundamental change comes only through God's grace.

Perhaps the most significant principle to maintain in outlining a theology of the kingdom of God is that the face Christians anticipate seeing on the throne on the last day is the face they have already seen on the cross on Good Friday. In other words, Jesus is as much the centre of Christian hope as he is the centre of Christian memory. The danger of overemphasizing the drama of what God has in store is that it diminishes the definitive character of what has already been revealed in Christ. Meanwhile if both the definitive significance of Christ in the past and the final revelation of God in the future are downplayed, the inevitable outcome is the exaltation of human endeavour in the present. Anglican spirituality has most often ensured that the centre of attention has remained not on the moment of personal conversion nor on the moment of death or the last day, but instead squarely on the days of Christ's birth, crucifixion and resurrection. Here again is an indication of what an Anglican emphasis on the incarnation implies.

One characteristic way in which Anglicans have focused on the future, coming and entirely God-initiated dimension of the kingdom of God is by dwelling, through liturgy and preaching, in the season of Advent, on the 'four last things' – death, judgement, heaven and hell. These are the future ways in which God resolves all that is not right with the world and completes the story begun in creation. When the term kingdom is spoken of in the present tense, what is not right with the world is broadly resolved into two dimensions: that which has a human cause (often described as oppression or injustice) and that which does not (and yet is still experienced as suffering). The response to both dimensions is rooted in Jesus' ministry. When injustice seems evident, attention dwells upon Jesus' frequent controversies with the Jerusalem authorities and the way he endorsed and imitated the prophetic ministry of John the Baptist and before him figures such as Amos and Jeremiah, who had called for Israel to demonstrate faithfulness to God by showing mercy to the stranger, the orphan and the widow. When less culpable suffering is more prevalent, the focus turns to Jesus' healing ministry, particularly the way it reached out to those beyond the bounds of conventional respectability, such as the woman with haemorrhages (Mark 5.25–29) or the Samaritan leper (Luke 17.11–19).

The parable of the last judgement (Matt. 25.31–46) suggests that in the end no firm line may be drawn between disorder that comes from human hand and that which does not. The work of the kingdom is to recognize and meet Jesus in the hungry, thirsty, stranger, naked, sick or prisoner, not to make distinctions based on how a person came to be so. Such convictions have underwritten widespread charitable work in the Anglican Communion, almost all of which can be read as a response to one or more dimensions of this parable and its clear message.

In short, the kingdom of God refers to the way the ministry of Christ and the blessing of the Holy Spirit stretches to the bounds of creation, whether through or in spite of the mission of the Church.

Salvation

The axis of the Christian faith is how God infuses the disorder of human life in such a way that not only humanity but also the whole creation is redeemed. This redemption has several aspects: the nature of humanity and the nature of the flaws in humanity; the way in which Christ's life, death and resurrection transforms human potential and reality; the ways in which this transformation is received; the nature of human flourishing in the power of the Spirit; humankind's ultimate destiny; and the question of whether and to what extent Jesus of Nazareth is the single, central or indispensable part of this process.

The dignity of humankind resides in that we were the dimension of created existence God chose to assume and embrace in becoming incarnate in Jesus Christ. Thus the key characteristics of human nature are those shared with Jesus; those not shared with Jesus – notably sin – are not inherent and integral to human identity. Genesis 1.27 describes how 'God created humankind in his image, in the image of God he created them; male and female he created them.' This has raised a wide variety of interpretations through the centuries about the sense in which humankind bears God's image. Some have seen the image as constituted by the capacity to reason; others by the extent of freedom; others again by the authority delegated in Genesis 1.28 to 'fill the earth and subdue it; and have dominion over the fish of the sea and over the birds of the air and over every living thing that moves upon the earth'. But each of these is fulfilled in the coming of Christ who, as Colossians 1.15–16 declares, is 'the image of the invisible God, the firstborn of all creation; for in him all things in heaven and on earth were created, things visible and invisible, whether thrones or dominions or rulers or powers – all things have been created through him and for him'. There is no 'sanctity of life', as such: there is the sanctity of God, and human life is sacred in that God created it and has chosen to be in relationship with it, most fully and demonstrably in Jesus.

What might it look like for humanity to flourish? One picture that portrays God's destiny for humanity is that offered in Isaiah 65.17–25. Here God speaks of taking 'delight in my people'; God promises that 'no more shall there be in [Jerusalem] an infant that lives but a few days, or an old person who does not live out a lifetime'. God foresees that 'They shall build houses and inhabit them; they shall plant vineyards and eat their fruit.' God intends that 'they shall not labour in vain' and even that 'the wolf and the lamb shall feed together', because 'They shall not hurt or destroy on all my holy mountain.' This is a vision of health and well-being, of security, justice and demanding but fulfilling and fruitful labour, and healthy relationships between people and each other, people and animals and people and the soil. This is a comprehensive picture of many dimensions of flourishing life. The one dimension perhaps missing here that the Old Testament as a whole emphasizes, is worship. A healthy human life is one that worships God aright and in so doing finds its place among all things and sets each in their proper station. But crucial to Isaiah's vision is that this flourishing life is what gives God joy: 'I am about to create Jerusalem as a *joy*, and its people as a *delight*. I will *rejoice* in Jerusalem, and *delight* in my people' (Isa. 65.18–19; emphasis added).

One way in which contemporary Anglican belief has altered from understandings widely held for much of the Church of England's history is in the notion of what constitutes diverse persons' proper station. Once it was quite common to understand women as subject to men, particularly in marriage; to understand slavery as acceptable, even fitting; to understand children as potentially wild and needing to be tamed; and to understand the rich and the poor as assigned to their proper stations in life, perhaps even by God. It is usual today to reject

such understandings and to perceive them as signs of humanity gone astray rather than humanity flourishing. Indeed many
Anglicans sense that it is precisely in the challenging and
overcoming of such social structures that Christian mission
explicitly lies.

For all the goodness of God's creation and the richness of
God's will for human flourishing, all is not well with humanity
and its relationship with God and the creation. The Thirty-
Nine Articles are uncompromising in their estimation of the
human condition: 'man is very far gone from original righteousness, and is of his own nature inclined to evil, so that the
flesh lusteth always contrary to the spirit; and therefore in
every person born into this world, it deserveth God's wrath
and damnation' (Article IX). Such a far-reaching estimation of
human failure requires some more nuanced delineation of the
symptoms and causes of sin.

Sin is living as if there were no God, no grace of God, no
creation to remember or kingdom to hope for, no forgiveness to redeem the past or eternal life to focus the future, no
faith, no hope, no love. It is living outside the narrative of God
– without regard to the creation, the covenant with Israel,
the revelation in Christ, the existence of the Church, the consummation on the last day – and making one's own narrative
instead. Sin comes in two broad forms. On the one hand it
arises from ignorance, immaturity, foolishness, lack of insight,
clumsiness, hastiness, laziness and a host of shortcomings that
could eventually be ameliorated through thoughtfulness, formation, education, wisdom and patience. On the other hand it
is utterly perverse and inexplicable: it is the turning from glory
to sordidness, joy to meanness, beauty to tawdriness, grace
to misery. The first kind of sin is a failure of the imagination
– failure to enter and enjoy and inhabit the wondrous world
made possible by creation, covenant and Christ. The second
kind of sin is sheer perversity: however propitious the circumstances, blessed the surroundings, generous the provision or
abundant the resources, humankind will somehow contrive
to ruin things. The first kind means people get things wrong

however hard they try; the second recognizes that some of the time an element within every person has no intention of getting things right.

The simplest summary of the covenant with God offered in the Scriptures is Jesus' summary of the Law: '"You shall love the Lord your God with all your heart, and with all your soul, and with all your mind." This is the greatest and first commandment. And a second is like it: "You shall love your neighbour as yourself"' (Matt. 22.37–39). Here is the essence of the Christian life: to love God, your neighbour and yourself. Not wholly to love God is seldom to enter a world without love; more often it is wholly to love something that is not God – to make a god out of something that did not create and cannot save. This is known as idolatry. Not to love your neighbour is sometimes to fail to trust that God has made adequate provision for both you and your neighbour – that there is enough, and that your own flourishing need not involve your neighbour's diminishing. The fear of scarcity is near the root of many forms of sin. But not loving the neighbour can also take a more subtle form. It can be to fail to love yourself, allowing or encouraging your neighbour to take advantage of or oppress you when you should have every reason to stand your ground. The 1662 and the 1979 Book of Common Prayer express this twofold dimension of sin by expressing confession as follows: 'We have left undone those things that we ought to have done; and we have done those things that we ought not to have done.'[10]

Augustine of Hippo (354–430) made a helpful distinction between those things we 'enjoy' and those things we 'use'.[11] Those things we enjoy never run out and are an abundant blessing. They are an end in themselves, and to be with them is to be with God. (For Augustine God alone was to be enjoyed; I am developing his ideas somewhat here.) Those things we use are largely a means to an end. They do run out and they are

---

10 Church of England, *Common Worship: Services and Prayers for the Church of England* (London: Church House Publishing, 2000), p. 129.

11 Augustine, *On Christian Doctrine*, Book 1, chapters 3, 4 (trans. J. F. Shaw, Edinburgh: T&T Clark, 1892), p. 9.

not things we should set our hearts on. Their value is to help us reach, prepare for, value and understand the things that we are to enjoy. A simple way to describe sin is therefore as follows: to sin is to enjoy things that should properly only be used; and meanwhile merely to use things that should properly be enjoyed. The former is known as idolatry; the latter is ingratitude. In this sense it is easier to see how the noblest act may bear traces of sin because, short of heaven, scarcely anyone learns how fully to enjoy – and the perverse impulse to use is ineradicable.

How does Jesus save us? The Nicene Creed makes no attempt to answer this often-controversial question – it simply says that 'for us and for our salvation' Jesus Christ 'came down from heaven' and was born, lived, suffered, was buried, rose again and is seated at the right hand of the Father, whence he will come again to judge and rule forever. Broadly five answers to this question have gained wide influence among Anglicans.[12]

One emphasizes Jesus' birth. Jesus saves us by 'recapitulating' or re-enacting each aspect of our human existence, setting it right as if it were a broken bone. Adam disobeyed God by eating from the tree; Christ obeyed God by dying on the tree. Christ restores every dimension of human life. We are saved because Christ transforms the corruptible, finite quality of human nature by harnessing it to the immortal, incorruptible character of God. Christ also transforms death, in the crucifixion and resurrection – but the incarnation itself is the real moment of salvation.

A second answer emphasizes Jesus' life. It considers humankind as the audience for Jesus' life. In his kindness and generosity, his ministry to outcasts, sinners and the sick, his close relationship to the Father, his prophetic confrontation with those who kept people under oppression and most of all in his selfless and faithful journey to the cross, Jesus offers himself as the one who transforms our hearts to follow in his steps in the way of sacrificial love. Jesus doesn't seem objectively

---

12 The following paragraphs closely follow a longer treatment in Samuel Wells, *Speaking the Truth*, pp. 155–61.

to change anything about fundamental reality, rather it is we who are changed. Thus this theory is sometimes described as subjective.

A third approach focuses on the suffering laid on Jesus as he went to and hung on the cross. This theory assumes the setting of a court of law. Humanity, the defendant, had accumulated an unpayable level of guilt before God. Humanity therefore deserved eternal punishment. But through a unique act of grace, God sent Jesus to face this punishment in our place. This is often called penal substitution. While his death is significant and the resurrection is not ignored, the theory rests so much on the necessity of punishment that attention often focuses chiefly on the extent of Jesus' sufferings because it is they rather than his death that substitute for the sins of the whole world.

A fourth perspective looks more precisely to Jesus' death itself. Jesus is a sacrifice that sets right our relationship to God. In this view the problem is essentially one of debt. The most influential view says that the debt is to God's honour. The failure of humanity to do justice before God creates a terrible imbalance in the moral universe. Only humanity *must* pay the debt but only God *can* pay the debt. Hence the God-human, Jesus. When Jesus dies he repays the debt of honour with interest, and it is this interest, known as merit, that humanity can access through the sacraments and thus find salvation. This is a characteristically Roman Catholic view. An older version of this theory also focused on Jesus' actual death but saw the debt as owed not to God but to Satan. In this view Adam and Eve had sold humanity to the devil and thus God needed to ransom humanity the way one would redeem a slave. However, Jesus' death, while succeeding as a ransom and buying us back, was in fact a trick because Jesus rose from death and escaped the devil's clutches. Most uses of the word redemption hint at this ransom theory.

A fifth answer dwells on Jesus' resurrection. If substitution sees salvation as decided in a law court, then this fifth view sees it as a battle. Death cannot hold Jesus; he destroys death and opens out the prospect of eternal life by rising from the grave.

The resurrection of Jesus brings about our resurrection by dismantling the hold of death not just once but for all time. The key word is victory. This is the characteristic Eastern Orthodox view. It has achieved a revival in some parts of the Anglican Communion, particularly among those keen to stress how Jesus' resurrection saves not just the individual soul but transforms whole societies by dismantling all the social, economic and cultural forces that oppress people.

One problem with each of these answers is their abstract character and the way they elide the details of Jesus' life, most notably his Jewishness. An approach that has become influential in Anglican theology in recent times, and focuses on precisely these details, is to observe how Jesus in his ministry brought people out of exile – death, sickness, social exclusion, fear – and overall brought Israel out of the exile that she had been in for 500 years. This is a vision of salvation that emphasizes the corporate over the individual and offers a greater role for the Church.

Two terms associated closely with Reformation debates concerning salvation are justification and sanctification. No fewer than seven of the Thirty-Nine Articles are given over to justification. These articles carefully outline how Jesus enables believers to stand before God without fear. There is nothing human beings can do to earn salvation: 'We are accounted righteous before God, only for the merit of our Lord and Saviour Jesus Christ by Faith, and not for our own works or deservings' (Article XI). The attempt to live a holy life is fruitless in terms of salvation, but is a sign of gratitude and a healthy desire to imitate Christ:

Albeit that Good Works, which are the fruits of Faith, and follow after Justification, cannot put away our sins, and endure the severity of God's Judgement; yet are they pleasing and acceptable to God in Christ, and do spring out necessarily of a true and lively Faith insomuch that by them a lively Faith may be as evidently known as a tree discerned by the fruit. (Article XII)

33

But the works of a non-believer count for nothing in terms of justification and 'are not pleasant to God': indeed 'for that they are not done as God hath willed and commanded them to be done, we doubt not but they have the nature of sin' (Article XIII). These rather austere articles emphasize the centrality of Christ for salvation. Only Christ is without sin; however worthy human works may be, they do not fit anyone to stand before God; salvation is therefore an act of pure divine grace and in no sense a human achievement. Yet humans should nonetheless strive to lead a holy life – not as an attempt to secure salvation (which only Christ can do, on their behalf) but in reverence for, gratitude towards and imitation of Jesus.

Our earlier distinction between perversity and lack of imagination may help to clarify the concerns of the Articles. When it comes to lack of imagination, the work of the Holy Spirit may gradually heal, transform, amend, refine and purify human lives, such that they may be made holy. This is the process known as sanctification. It receives very little attention in the Thirty-Nine Articles and is associated less with Anglicanism than with Methodism. But perversity is something that can only be addressed by Christ, most specifically in his single sacrificial act on the cross and its transformation through his resurrection. Thus justification, which addresses perversity, is a past achievement of Jesus Christ to which Christians may give their present assent in baptism and sincere declarations of repentance and faith; whereas sanctification is a present and future process, shaped by the activity of the Holy Spirit within the believer and issuing in the fruits of the Spirit: 'love, joy, peace, patience, kindness, generosity, faithfulness, gentleness, and self-control' (Gal. 5.22–23).

Short of eternal life, what does redeemed existence look like? In addition to the well-being, secure labour, healthy relationships and joyful worship we saw in our earlier discussion of Isaiah 65, perhaps two further dimensions stand out. One is forgiveness. The fruits of redemption are forgiveness and eternal life. Forgiveness restores the past; eternal life opens out the future. Forgiveness is simply one aspect of a whole series of steps through which God's action in Christ, received through the Holy Spirit, makes it possible for the past to be restored. While the rite of reconciliation, commonly known as 'making one's confession', is not universally practised in the Anglican Communion, it does offer a structure for thinking about forgiveness. The priest reminds the penitent sinner of God's longing to welcome prodigal children home and the rejoicing of the angels at every sinner who repents. The sinner is then invited to tell a truthful story about the past, express remorse, commit to setting right what has been put wrong and seek to avoid repeating such offences in future. The priest then offers counsel, striving to find wisdom in even the most wayward of wanderings. The priest also suggests a penance, a concrete act by which the contrite penitent may express regret and begin to enter new life. Then the priest offers words of forgiveness. Reconciliation is thus made with God, but it is up to penitents to make reconciliation with those they have harmed. This process of trust–truthtelling–penitence–forgiveness–reconciliation portrays the way that forgiveness, rather than being an event, names a process that begins with the proclamation of grace and ends with its fruit.

A second dimension of redeemed existence is the discovery, reception and exploration of vocation. Vocation is closely tied to baptism: in baptism the past is redeemed by the forgiveness of sins and the future is extended in the promise of eternal life; but also the more immediate future is offered in the commissioning to a vocation. A vocation is a particular calling from God through which believers find their own place in the story of the redemption of all things. It is not necessarily tied or even closely related to the duties of a job or the pursuit of a career. It is not necessarily static and permanent: it may develop and evolve over time. But it is tailored to a person's unique character and circumstances and it invariably involves synthesizing the disparate and sometimes confusing elements of a person's past experiences into a role only they can perform, a gift only they can give, a contribution only they can make. And in a general way that role is called ministry, both because ministry primarily means service and, in the words of the collect, God's 'service is perfect freedom', and because all ministry derives from Christ's ministry and thus Christ's ministry becomes a template for all vocation. Vocations must therefore be expected to take on key characteristics of Christ's ministry – his mission to reconcile all people to God, his willingness to face suffering and sacrifice, his presence among a close community of believers, among the poor and in intense dialogue with the powers of his day. A true vocation blends the uniqueness of the believer's character and circumstance with the universal claims of Christ.

But what of *eternal* salvation – what of heaven and hell?[13] Neither the creeds nor the Thirty-Nine Articles offer any details on the life of heaven. The important things to keep in mind about heaven are that it is shaped by the Trinitarian God met in Christ; that it is embodied rather than simply spiritual; and that it is dynamic rather than static.

To say heaven is shaped by Christ is to dismiss popular and folk conceptions of heaven contained in lines such as 'I am a thousand winds that blow' or 'I have simply passed into the next room'. Heaven is not human survival; it is the new life received as a pure gift after true and complete death and physical resurrection. The death and resurrection of Christ provides the paradigm for the death and resurrection of the believer: in other words, the resurrected body may be expected to bear the scars of wounds received before death but also to be a body restored and a physical and mental state of being unburdened of the pain of those scars. Death is real: Christ's resurrection removes its sting but not its universality. Resurrection is not reabsorption into the infinite: it is distinct, personal existence. Heaven is not the resumption of earthly everyday life: it is a state of restored, renewed and fulfilled relationship with God and one another.

The three most explicit scriptural depictions of heaven are as worship, friendship and the sharing of food. Images of a banquet abound in the Scriptures and affirm the physical, con-

---

13 For a longer treatment of these issues see Wells, *Speaking the Truth*, pp. 143–55.

vivial and corporate nature of resurrection. Companionship with God, so clearly depicted in the risen Jesus' walk with two grieving disciples on the road to Emmaus (Luke 24), is a restoration of what was lost in the fall. Yet the central image of heaven is that of enjoying and glorifying God forever – like a choir of diverse voices harmonized in song, each member finding their true fulfilment in a chorus that transcends their individual callings.

There are two broad notions of hell: everlasting agony or total annihilation. The first idea, of perpetual torment, picks up on a good deal of scriptural imagery and maintains the physical dimension of life after death. The second idea, of endless isolation and the utter absence of God, tends to see hell as the complete evacuation of the good and the real. However, both accounts are problematic when set against the two key attributes of God, namely all-loving and all-powerful. If God is all-loving, how could there be eternal punishment for temporal sin? And if God is all-powerful, how could there be a sphere of existence that perpetually refuses to inhabit the economy of grace? How can there be an eternal estrangement from God that Jesus has not addressed? The Thirty-Nine Articles are at pains to dispel the 'Romish Doctrine concerning Purgatory' which, among other notions, it describes as 'a fond thing, vainly invented, and grounded upon no warranty of Scripture, but rather repugnant to the Word of God' (Article XXII). Yet it is hard to do justice to the scriptural imagery of fire and torment and gnashing of teeth, the belief that Jesus displays the character of God and the conviction that God achieved everything in Jesus, without some notion that Jesus in his suffering on the cross transforms the ugliness of human sin into the beauty of God's grace; and that this is a more demanding and laborious process for some sinners than it is for others. Many contemporary versions of the Apostles' Creed omit any reference to hell; meanwhile the Nicene Creed speaks only of 'the resurrection of the dead, and the life of the world to come', with no specific reference to damnation. That reticence has become the custom in many parts of the Anglican Communion. Yet removing the crucial moment of God's judgement from the believer's anticipation of death has a significant side effect. The longing for human flourishing and well-being is transferred towards this present life. This motivates humanitarian movements concerned to enhance the living conditions of all human beings. But it also changes the sense of death from being 'but the step to life immortal',[14] in the words of the Easter hymn, to the last incongruous insult in a catalogue of apparent injustices that hold human beings back from the ultimate and perpetual earthly fulfilment they take to be their birthright.

In plural religious cultures, Christians will always be sensitive to the question of whether Jesus is the only way to salvation. This question tends to dominate interreligious dialogue and evoke passionate and polarized convictions. On the one hand, it seems out of character for the God of grace and generosity to withhold eternal well-being from not just infants or those who have never had a chance to hear the gospel, but also those who have been faithful adherents of other faiths and those who have sought to live what Titus 1.8 calls an 'upright and sober life'. On the other hand, the New Testament assumes that salvation has come uniquely through Jesus, and that is the power and urgency of its evangelistic message. The Thirty-Nine Articles are uncompromising on this point: 'Holy Scripture doth set out unto us only the Name of Jesus Christ, whereby men must be saved' (Article XXVIII). Moreover so much of St Paul's teaching emphasizes that God does not judge human beings on the quality of their lives but looks instead to the comprehensiveness of Jesus' offering and the transparency of the believer's faith. Such ambivalence has meant that this question has not received a clear answer in the present generation.

But the key is to keep the emphasis on what heaven *is* rather than on who gets there. If heaven is God's gift of everlasting security and well-being and interdependent growth and flourishing, then that is evidently God's will for all creation. But if

---

14 Jesus lives! henceforth is death / But the gate of life immortal; / This shall calm our trembling breath, / When we pass its gloomy portal. Alleluia! (from the hymn 'Jesus lives!' by Christian Furchtegott Gellert).

heaven is more than that, if heaven is intimate companionship with God in Christ, a shape of life made possible by Jesus' cross and resurrection and expressed in worship and the sharing of food, then it is hard to see why anyone who wanted that in the eternal future would not want it in the present too.

2 The Sources of the Faith

Introduction: Revelation and Authority

How does the Trinity that shapes its life to be in relationship to human beings come to be known and understood and loved by them? How is an account such as that offered in the previous chapter arrived at, and on what grounds is any person to trust such an account as more than a fanciful rendering of reality? These are questions of revelation and authority. The characteristic Anglican answers to these questions are the subject of this second part of our study.

Revelation refers to the unveiling of the person, character and purpose of God. Each term in this definition may be explored further.

By 'unveiling' is meant the more complete disclosure of the already apparent God. It is customary to distinguish between two forms of this disclosure. On the one hand there is natural (sometimes known as general) revelation; on the other there is special revelation, which indicates all that is not accessible except through the eyes of faith. Anglican theologians have been more inclined than many others to attend to natural revelation. The empirical tradition in English philosophy, which favours observation, experimentation and experience, coupled with the pragmatic tradition in American philosophy, which perceives the meaning of a concept in the practical outcomes of adhering to it, steer Anglican theology towards the tangible signs of divine expression. There is good precedent for such convictions in the Bible: Psalm 19.1–2 declares, 'The heavens are telling the glory of God; and the firmament proclaims his handiwork. Day to day pours forth speech, and night to night declares knowledge.' The Old Testament figure Job is constantly scouring the creation for signs of God's benevolent hand, declaring:

He is wise in heart, and mighty in strength – who has resisted him, and succeeded? – he who removes mountains, and they do not know it, when he overturns them in his anger; who shakes the earth out of its place, and its pillars tremble; who commands the sun, and it does not rise; who seals up the stars . . . who does great things beyond understanding, and marvellous things without number . . . who can stop him? (Job 9.4–12)

And in the New Testament Paul bases his argument among the Athenians around identifying the God whom they already know but have not yet named (Acts 17.22–32).

On the other hand revealed theology, or special revelation as it is sometimes called, directs attention to the specific characteristics of God that are not generally accessible to the ordinary human senses. These include identifying God as Trinity, the naming of the three persons of the Trinity as Father, Son and Holy Spirit, the incarnation of Jesus Christ, the life of the Church in the power of the Holy Spirit, the form and process of salvation and the hope of everlasting life with God.

The threefold formulation 'Scripture, tradition and reason' is the characteristic Anglican model for perceiving revelation and understanding authority. The crucial point to grasp about this understanding of revelation is that in the customary formulation of Scripture, tradition and reason, *all three* are regarded as forms of revelation, as this chapter seeks to demonstrate. It is not that Scripture comprises revelation, tradition describes implementation and reason amasses all the questions or new information that are in tension with Scripture and tradition. It is that Scripture, tradition and reason constitute complementary and overlapping sources of revelation. They are not inherently in tension with one another – they are three dimensions of the way the Church discovers and rediscovers who God is, what is

God's purpose for creation and what is made possible by God's redemption in Christ.

One common contemporary configuration is to add the term 'experience' as a fourth dimension in addition to Scripture, tradition and reason. But this is based on a misunderstanding of Scripture, tradition and reason themselves. None of these three forms of revelation is self-explanatory in itself: each comes to be understood as it is interpreted in the life of a community of faith. In other words, experience is simply another name for the interpretative process by which the Church comes to receive revelation from Scripture, tradition and reason. To set experience up as a fourth source of authority is immediately to assume a tension between it and one or more of the previous three. Instead experience should be regarded as an aspect of Scripture in that Scripture was recorded, collected and edited by communities of faith as they experienced the work of the Holy Spirit; tradition means the distilled history and wisdom of communities seeking to embody Scripture; and reason refers to the ways communities have sought to translate their knowledge of the world into the language of Scripture, and their knowledge of Scripture into the language of the world. In other words, all three emerged, and are still emerging, in gradual dialogue with experience. This emphasis on communal discernment is vital to the understanding of revelation and authority. Prayer is common, corporate prayer, and discernment of Scripture – the principal authority – takes place in the context of this common prayer. Thus the English theologian Richard Hooker (1554–1600), the most cited source on these matters in the Anglican tradition, describes the process for coming to a common mind on matters about which Scripture is silent or unclear. He says that if there is a consensus of persons of moderate judgement, who believe that proposed readings are neither unjust nor unreasonable; and that those readings of Scripture promote godliness, have been sanctioned by long tradition in the Church or have been approved by the legitimate authority of the Church; then the community should affirm those readings. A key test of this approach came when The Episcopal Church was founded after the Revolutionary War and decisions needed to be made concerning how it should understand authority. It committed itself to having bishops, and to a set form of common prayer, while remaining open to local variation in matters 'inessential' that did not contradict Scripture.[1]

One scriptural story that illuminates the relationship between natural and revealed theology is Matthew's account of the birth of Jesus (2.1–12). The wise men beheld a star in the heavens: here is the language of natural revelation. They responded and made their way to Jerusalem. Thus it is possible to be drawn towards God without Scripture. The wise men were close to the truth of Christ's birth – but a miss was as good as a mile. Without Scripture it is not possible to know the heart of God, to meet the incarnate Jesus. When the wise men came to Jerusalem the scribes explored the Scriptures and found that the Messiah was to be born in Bethlehem: here is a moment of special revelation. The wise men then made their way to Bethlehem, to find something natural revelation could never have disclosed: a vulnerable baby, born in humble circumstances yet proclaimed as the Son of God. The story thus portrays the two kinds of revelation harmoniously balanced in bringing people face to face with God. It offers a model for Christian understandings of other forms of knowledge, such as science, and of other forms of faith, such as Islam and Buddhism. The lesson of the story of the wise men is that general revelation may get one to 'Jerusalem'; only special revelation may get one that short but crucial extra step to 'Bethlehem'.

How does revelation take place? This is one of the most pressing questions for many Christians seeking to discover and respond obediently to God's character and will. One may speak of four modes, or moments, of revelation, each of which is extensively exhibited in Scripture.

1 Attention inevitably settles upon momentary, dramatic, divine interventions. There are many such moments in Scrip-

---

1 I am grateful to Craig Uffman for helping me clarify the thoughts in this paragraph.

ture, several of which are associated with the call of a prophet or servant of God. In the Old Testament perhaps the most vivid moment occurs when fingers appear at the feast of the Chaldean King Belshazzar and write words on the wall, which Daniel interprets to mean the king will be overthrown that very night (Dan. 5.1–30). Another example is that of Elijah who, when hiding on Mount Horeb, did not find God in the earthquake, the wind or the fire but in the ensuing sound of an echoing silence (1 Kings 19.11–18). One striking event in the New Testament is the appearance of the angel Gabriel to Mary, announcing that she will bear a son (Luke 1.26–38). Perhaps the definitive among such moments is the account of the conversion of Paul on the road to Damascus, when:

suddenly a light from heaven flashed around him. He fell to the ground and heard a voice saying to him, 'Saul, Saul . . . I am Jesus, whom you are persecuting' . . . Saul got up from the ground, and though his eyes were open, he could see nothing; so they led him by the hand and brought him into Damascus. For three days he was without sight, and neither ate nor drank . . . Ananias . . . laid his hands on Saul and said, 'Brother Saul, the Lord Jesus, who appeared to you on your way here, has sent me so that you may regain your sight and be filled with the Holy Spirit.' And immediately something like scales fell from his eyes, and his sight was restored. Then he got up and was baptized. (Acts 9.3–18)

Stories of similar intensity have continued to be told throughout the history of the Church. But they have never been considered normative for all other forms of revelation. Three other dimensions of divine disclosure stand alongside the dramatic form.

2 One is the carefully established, regular and habitual forms of embodied devotion, such as personal and corporate prayer and worship, Scripture study, pilgrimage, fasting and being present among the poor, prisoners, the sick and the dying. These are places where the faithful may expect to come face to face with

God, consciously or unconsciously. An example of the conscious confrontation with God during a regular act of piety is Zechariah's experience when he was chosen by lot to enter the temple sanctuary and offer incense. An angel appeared and announced that Zechariah and his wife Elizabeth were to have a son named John (Luke 1.5–23). An example of unconscious divine encounter is described by Jesus in his parable of the last judgement:

> Then the righteous will answer him, 'Lord, when was it that we saw you hungry and gave you food, or thirsty and gave you something to drink? And when was it that we saw you a stranger and welcomed you, or naked and gave you clothing? And when was it that we saw you sick or in prison and visited you?' And the king will answer them, 'Truly I tell you, just as you did it to one of the least of these who are members of my family, you did it to me.' (Matt. 25.37–40)

The gathering of councils of the Church is one of the 'regular' places where revelation may be expected; the gatherings of the early ecumenical councils, where the creeds were articulated, are assigned a special authority.

3 Another significant way in which revelation is disclosed is through retrospection. Sometimes a pattern can appear when a series of historical events are set alongside one another – a pattern that was not so apparent when these events were taking place. In the Old Testament, Psalm 78 offers an ordered sequence of acts of God that create a cumulative message describing God's purpose and faithfulness. In the New Testament (Hebrews 11) a similar litany of blessing is outlined in the series of those who acted by faith.

4 The fourth and ultimate form of revelation is the full disclosure of God on the last day, a prospect anticipated at many places in the New Testament and most amply in the book of Revelation. This vision is rendered vividly in the words of Charles Wesley's Advent hymn:

Every eye shall now behold Him
Robed in dreadful majesty;
Those who set at naught and sold Him,
Pierced and nailed Him to the tree,
Deeply wailing, deeply wailing,
Shall the true Messiah see.[2]

The Church of England was born amid a crisis of authority: the Reformation pitted the custom of ancient tradition and vested office against the appeal to Scripture alone. Placing Scripture first in the threefold formula is a significant gesture to the Protestant side of this Reformation debate. But by following Scripture with tradition, Anglicans make a similar nod in a Catholic direction. Just as the Reformation made it problematic to assert tradition over Scripture, so the Enlightenment severely criticized inherited authority (and thus both Scripture and tradition), preferring to prize reason above all things. By including reason in their threefold formula, Anglicans acknowledge the challenge of the Enlightenment but make a statement that there is no reason that arises in the abstract: every question, every critical enquiry arises out of some kind of tradition.

Scripture

The Thirty-Nine Articles make a confident statement about which books constitute Holy Scripture. 'In the name of the Holy Scripture we do understand those canonical Books of the Old and New Testament, of whose authority was never any doubt in the Church' (Article VI). By 'never any doubt' the Articles refer to the process of reception by which the early Church came to recognize the books of the Old Testament and the New – a process largely complete in the late second century. (There was plenty of doubt before that!) The exact list was not finalized – to include Jude, 2 Peter and 1, 2 and 3 John – until the fourth century. The authoritative books are known

---

2 'Lo, he comes with clouds descending'.

as the canon – coming originally from an Egyptian word meaning 'reed', and coming more broadly to mean 'rule' or 'norm'. The make-up of the New Testament ceased to be a source of controversy in the fourth century: while there exist a number of writings from the first two centuries that describe the life of Christ or list sayings or reflections, such as the Epistle of Barnabas or the Shepherd of Hermas, these have not been regarded as authoritative.

One controversial and unresolved area concerns which books, precisely, constitute the Old Testament. The 39 Jewish books that are written in Hebrew form the undisputed Old Testament; meanwhile Greek versions of the Old Testament (the Septuagint) include 11–14 additional Jewish books written in Greek, which were excluded by most Jews from AD 90 onwards. These books, which came to be known collectively as the Apocrypha ('hidden away'), were generally recognized by the whole Church prior to the Reformation but have not been considered canonical by most Protestant traditions since. In a characteristic compromise, the Thirty-Nine Articles name two additional books, 1 and 2 Esdras, among the books of the Old Testament, and then list the rest of the pre-New Testament books separately, accompanied by the phrase, 'the other Books . . . the Church doth read for example of life and instruction of manners; but yet doth it not apply them to establish any doctrine' (Article VI). These books are usually printed separately from the Old Testament books, and some congregations read them occasionally in worship in place of the Old Testament lesson. One error the Thirty-Nine Articles are quick to quell is any suggestion that the Old Testament lacks authority, having been superseded by the New in the coming of Christ. The articles insist, 'The Old Testament is not contrary to the New: for both in the Old and New Testament everlasting life is offered to Mankind by Christ' (Article VII). Anglican theology makes no concession to the notion that the Old Testament God is a God of war, rule or tribe, in contrast with the New Testament God of peace, grace and everyone. Rather the Old Testament *is* the gospel, and God speaks in, through and from it. However, a more subtle approach is employed in relation to the very large numbers of rules and commandments offered in the Torah (the first five books of the Old Testament). Following the twelfth-century Jewish scholar Maimonides, and in keeping with much Reformation thought, the Articles make the following distinction:

> Although the Law given from God by Moses, as touching Ceremonies and Rites, do not bind Christian men, nor the Civil precepts thereof ought of necessity to be received in any commonwealth; yet notwithstanding, no Christian man whatsoever is free from the obedience of the Commandments which are called Moral. (Article VII)

This distinction between the moral, ceremonial and civil commandments is widely upheld today, although disputes arise as to which category certain commandments (such as some of those pertaining to sexual expression) truly belong, and the distinction itself relies on an anachronistic division of categories unknown to the Old Testament imagination. What is it that turns these particular written words into Holy Scripture? The notion of the authority of Scripture is a way of talking about two claims – and sometimes about a third less helpful assertion. What is really at stake is the authority of God. And that means that God is the source of all that is good, right, true and beautiful, the creator and sustainer of all things and the origin and destiny of everything dead, living and yet to be. The second and subsidiary claim is that the Bible is the unique and comprehensive witness to the God who has such authority. This is largely a claim about the inspiration of Scripture. But it also implies that the Bible gives us a way of reading all other forms of knowledge and discerning all other kinds of wisdom. One can, for example, see the Bible as telling a story in five parts – creation, covenant (with Israel), Christ, Church and consummation (the end of all things).[3] This story distils the witness of

---

3 For an extensive treatment of this notion of authority see Samuel Wells, *Improvisation: The Drama of Christian Ethics* (Grand Rapids, MI: Brazos and London: SPCK, 2004), especially pp. 53–7.

the Old and New Testaments and locates us, the Church, in the fourth part of a five-part narrative – thus giving us a sense of where we fit in God's purposes. The less helpful assertion is that Scripture has an authority that transcends (or excludes) all other authority – such as tradition or reason. Such an assumption neglects to recognize that every reading of Scripture is an act of interpretation that requires attention to earlier readings (tradition) and the wider discernment of the Church (reason). It is an assumption that tends to arise out of a legitimate fear that tradition or reason has strayed too far from Scripture itself. But it is an assertion that does not always direct attention to the authority of God the Trinity made known in Christ through the Holy Spirit in the world and in the Church.

If the question of authority partly, perhaps largely rests on a notion of inspiration, what then does it mean to regard the 39 books of the Old Testament and 27 books of the New as inspired? To speak of inspiration is to refer to the action of the Holy Spirit in regard to the Bible. There are three broad ways to conceive of scriptural inspiration. Since the Thirty-Nine Articles were first issued in 1563, the Bible has come under a host of new forms of scrutiny. Anglicans have in general been less discomfited by such kinds of criticism than most other Christians. The various forms of criticism, and responses to them, may be noted under their respective modes of scriptural inspiration.

1 One mode is to look behind the text to see inspiration in *the events the text describes*. Thus Moses and the children of Israel crossing the Red Sea is the important thing: the account of the event in Exodus 14–15 may or may not include some eccentricities and incongruities, but what matters is the event itself. This view sees the text as the best available witness to a series of uniquely inspired events and divine communications. It has difficulty adjusting to more complex parts of the Bible that make no claim to historical fact (such as the book of Job) because it is so tied to seeing Christianity as constituted by a sequence of historical events.

The major strength of this approach is that it has proved malleable in the face of a number of kinds of criticism. Thus source criticism attempts to identify the places or documents from which the scriptural authors derived their material (such as a notional text of Jesus' sayings that was available to Matthew and Luke but not to Mark); form criticism breaks the Scripture down into paragraphs or sections of various genres and speculates on the nature and pattern of those genres; while redaction criticism seeks to characterize the authors of the texts, their particular interests, the communities from which they arose and the needs they sought to meet by writing the texts. Meanwhile historians and archaeologists also seek to find evidence to corroborate or challenge the historical validity of texts that refer to specific events and persons.

These methods all seek to find the world *behind* the scriptural text. The empirical tradition in British thinking and the pragmatic tradition in American culture and philosophy both incline Anglicans and Episcopalians to be prepared to detach the scriptural accounts somewhat from the events they describe. This creates three dimensions instead of what had been one. That is to say, whereas there had once been only the event-as-recorded-in-Scripture, there is now, first, the event as witnessed by other authorities and partially reconstructed accordingly; second, the scriptural account (whose value goes far beyond a reduction to bare historical veracity, which is itself a relatively recent notion largely unknown to the scriptural authors); and third, the intersection between the two. Many find this complexity bewildering, and either long for or insist on a return to the one-dimensional conviction that Scripture is always a precise record of historical events. Nonetheless Anglican scholars in general have found a great deal of adaptability in becoming able to feel at home in all three of these dimensions.

2 A second understanding of inspiration is to look to the text itself to see inspiration in *the very words themselves*. Thus the psalms were inspired in their composition, and any reader who comes to them with a pure heart, ready to receive their wisdom,

may expect to glean from them abiding truth. Likewise if Jesus in one place says, 'Whoever is not against us is for us' (Mark 9.40), and in another place says, 'Whoever is not with me is against me' (Luke 11.23), the point is not to discover which of the sayings is the more likely to be historically attestable but to rest with both as authentic and authoritative. A strong version of this approach is to see the Scripture as infallible – in other words, to regard every word of the Scripture as equally sound and not to entertain any possibility that it might misrepresent history or misdirect future conduct. Another related assumption that is sometimes made is that the Bible is perspicuous – that is, that it has a single, plain meaning, and that this meaning is accessible to any reader in any context.

In scholarly terms the approach of looking at the text itself is associated with literary criticism, which considers the final form of the text without regard to authorial intent or textual emendations. Forms of literary criticism applied to the Bible include narrative criticism, which addresses plot, character and other such themes; rhetorical criticism, which studies the way a text shapes its audience; and canonical criticism, which considers the text in the light of the whole canon of Scripture of which it is a part.

3 A third perspective is to locate inspiration in *the life of a community that seeks to embody the text*. In this view the two things that matter most are the God of Jesus Christ and the faithfulness of those who seek to live the gospel. In other words, the precise details of the saving events and the sacred word – in short, the Bible – are not worth fighting over, because neither decisively shape what is more important: the character of God and the believer. Securing the authority of the exact words of Scripture is no guarantee of securing these vital elements of the faith. It is unusual to hold this perspective alone; more often it is combined with one or both of the previous approaches.

Those who adhere to the second view, that inspiration lies in the text itself, may be inclined to criticize proponents of the first and third perspectives on the grounds that they are treating the Bible as no more than a means to an end, and not giving the Scriptures the veneration they deserve. Advocates of the first and third approaches may counter that this is precisely how the Bible should be regarded – as a means, albeit perhaps the most significant means, to the end of meeting the God of Jesus Christ in historical revelation and in the Church today. To place higher value on the Scriptures than that, they might argue, is to risk making them the focus of idolatry, for it is God, not the Scriptures, that should be truly venerated. The most quoted verses in the debate are these: 'All scripture is inspired by God and is useful for teaching, for reproof, for correction, and for training in righteousness, so that everyone who belongs to God may be proficient, equipped for every good work' (2 Tim. 3.16–17). These verses can be adopted readily by proponents of each of the three views.

The characteristic Anglican approach has been to see wisdom in all three perspectives. While for much of Anglican history the sacredness of the text itself has been taken for granted, the fact that Anglicans have remained open to the first interpretation and, more recently, to the third, has meant that they have struggled less than many Protestant denominations over the last 150 years with the impact of historical and textual criticism of the Bible. A tradition that put all its emphasis on the inspiration of the words themselves would be much more vulnerable at points where the historical veracity or intratextual consistency of some of those words came to be questioned. By contrast, Anglicanism has generally held a broader notion of authority in relation to Scripture, and this has made it lighter on its feet in the face of such criticism.

One of the most famous lines in the Thirty-Nine Articles – echoed later in the Chicago-Lambeth Quadrilateral – runs as follows: 'Holy Scripture containeth all things necessary to salvation' (Article VI). This notion is known as the 'sufficiency' of Scripture. At first glance it might seem as though this statement contravenes the balance of Scripture, tradition and reason by placing all the emphasis on Scripture. But this is not the way it is usually interpreted. The point is that God has been fully revealed in Christ, and that Christ re-presents all that God made plain to Israel and discloses all creation that God has restored. There is nothing missing here. Any *addition* to what God has done in Christ would in fact be a *subtraction* because it would diminish the faith that God in Christ has done everything needful and more. Thus tradition and reason may amplify and clarify, order and embody what is disclosed in Scripture, but not add to, alter or contradict what is found there.

Anglicans have tended to take this notion of sufficiency in broad and general terms rather than precise and specific ones. Thus Scripture is taken as the witness of the shape of history – creation, covenant, Christ, Church, consummation; and the particular details of Christ's coming, death and resurrection – but the specifics, other than those concerning Christ, have been treated with less vigilant scrutiny. So it is, for example, normal for Anglicans today to regard the opening chapters of Genesis as a narrative that outlines God's originating purpose and human foolishness and fragility – and not to seek there a detailed historical account of universal or planetary origins, the nature of which may freely be sought among scholars of natural science. Likewise the book of Revelation and the second half of the book of Daniel are generally seen as a vivid challenge to the Church's relationship with ungodly power and a call to wait in hope for the coming of God's just, final and transforming reign. They are not regarded as a precise account of dispensatory stages towards the identification and preservation of an elect 144,000 souls as the rest of humanity thrashes and screams. When the Bible is used in Christian ethics, whether the subject be genetics or ecology or politics, the expectation is seldom that an exact prescription will be found for a pressing dilemma or crisis. Nonetheless the sufficiency of Scripture is witnessed in the expectation that – whether the theme is the goodness of creation, humanity made in the image of God, the Spirit's call to conversion, Christ's incarnational faithfulness with people of every kind and in every condition they find themselves, the cost of discipleship or the power of the resurrection – Scripture as discerned by the tradition and reason of the Church through the Holy Spirit will once again give God's people everything they need.

Tradition

The New Testament did not write itself or float down, complete and polished, from the sky. It was written by the early Church as its members were called to record the memories and practices of the apostles and the communities they founded in the power of the Spirit. Not only was Scripture tradition before it was Scripture, but elements of the earlier tradition are still visible in Scripture itself. For example, Paul's description of the humility of Christ (Phil. 2.6–11), which begins, 'who, though he was in the form of God, did not regard equality with God as something to be exploited, but emptied himself, taking the form of a slave, being born in human likeness', is widely regarded as deriving from an earlier hymn, not written by Paul but lodged in the tradition that emerged in the 25 years between the ascension of Christ and the writing of the Letter to the Philippians. Thus it was tradition, in the form of historical events, memories of Jesus, theological reflection and the reinterpretation of the Old Testament, that gave us Scripture.

But what is the status of tradition – or, better, traditions, for tradition is not and never could be a homogeneous unit – once the core of the tradition has been crystallized in the New Testament? This names one of the most controversial questions the Church has faced, one question that was at the heart of the Reformation. To answer it we need to offer a more complex account of what is meant by tradition. The traditions of the Church are those teachings and practices beyond but not necessarily in contradiction to the words of Scripture that have accumulated over the centuries and have stood the test of time. We may observe a number of kinds of these traditions.

One is the teachings and practices that go back to earliest times and seem to be more or less contemporaneous with the New Testament texts. Several prominent early Christian writers, such as Irenaeus, Tertullian and Origen, refer to a 'Rule of Faith' that was apparently in wide circulation but does not seem to have survived antiquity. The anthem widely sung in Eucharistic worship to the present day, which begins, 'Glory to God in the highest, and peace to his people on earth. Lord God, heavenly King, almighty God and Father, we worship you, we give you thanks, we praise you for your glory',[4] is one of several hymns from a similar period. Another such canticle, often sung at Morning Prayer, is known as the Te Deum. It begins, 'We praise thee, O God; we acknowledge thee to be the Lord.'[5] Also a very early text is the Apostles' Creed, which arose within the context of the liturgy of baptism but for which there is no known place or time or origin. Meanwhile the words, 'For thine is the kingdom, the power, and the glory, forever and ever. Amen', begin to appear appended to the Lord's Prayer in some later manuscripts of Matthew. While the central sacraments of baptism and Eucharist are explicitly cited in the New Testament, the elaborations of their celebration seem to be a similar very early development of the Church, and take their place alongside ancient developments not precisely recorded in Scripture but more or less complementary to the scriptural witness.

A second aspect of tradition refers to those teachings and practices that emerged more formally, especially those that did so during the undivided period in the Church's history, prior to the split between East and West in 1054, and in particular the seven ecumenical councils at which the whole Church was represented: Nicaea (325), Constantinople (381), Ephesus (431), Chalcedon (451), the Second Council of Constantinople (553), the Third Council of Constantinople (680) and the Second Council of Nicaea (787).[6] The creed of Nicaea (in the

---

4 *Common Worship: Services and Prayers for the Church of England*, p. 171.

5 *Common Worship: Services and Prayers for the Church of England*, p. 67.

6 The Roman Catholic Church recognizes a further 14 ecumenical councils, including the Fourth Lateran Council (1215), the Council of Trent (1545–63) and the Second Vatican Council (1965), but those have not tended to be given the same authority in Anglican circles.

form that emerged from the first council of Constantinople) and the definition of Chalcedon are the most explicit examples of this formal tradition. Whether the threefold order of ministry – bishop, priest and deacon – is visible in Scripture, or has emerged through informal or formal tradition, is a matter on which various opinions are held.

One document that offers a characteristic and influential understanding of tradition in the Anglican Communion is a statement on ecumenism issued by bishops of the Protestant Episcopal Church in the United States of America gathered in Chicago in 1886, subsequently distilled into Resolution 11 of the Lambeth Conference of all Anglican bishops in 1888 and henceforth known as the Chicago-Lambeth Quadrilateral. The Quadrilateral is an example of tradition as a dynamic, ongoing reality of faithful discernment, wisdom, experience and practice, as well as the process of reception by which the validity of tradition is established in the Church. In its latter form it regards the following four criteria (quoted here directly) as the basis for the reunion of the Churches:

(a) The Holy Scriptures of the Old and New Testaments, as 'containing all things necessary to salvation', and as being the rule and ultimate standard of faith.
(b) The Apostles' Creed, as the Baptismal Symbol; and the Nicene Creed, as the sufficient statement of the Christian faith.
(c) The two Sacraments ordained by Christ Himself – Baptism and the Supper of the Lord – ministered with unfailing use of Christ's words of Institution, and of the elements ordained by Him.
(d) The Historic Episcopate, locally adapted in the methods of its administration to the varying needs of the nations and peoples called of God into the Unity of His Church.

This succinctly summarizes what Anglicans mean by tradition and how that tradition sits alongside the authority of Scripture. But this is not all that tradition means. There are two further dimensions of the use of the term that need to be identified.

One is an almost technical term in that it is associated with the so-called Catholic Revival, whose most eloquent expression is found in the Oxford Movement within the Church of England beginning in the 1830s but with an influence that reaches up to the present day. When the Tractarians (as early members of this movement were known) employed the term 'tradition', they were referring explicitly to the revered works of the theologians of the first five centuries, whom they called, collectively, the 'Fathers'. These theologians may be grouped into three categories. There are the apostolic Fathers, who wrote around or shortly after the time of the composition of the New Testament (among them are Clement of Rome, Ignatius of Antioch and Polycarp). Then there are the eastern Fathers, who wrote in Greek (among them are Irenaeus, Clement of Alexandria, Origen, Athanasius, Basil of Caesarea, Gregory of Nazianzus and Gregory of Nyssa). Finally there are the western Fathers, who wrote in Latin (notably Tertullian, Ambrose, Augustine of Hippo and Gregory the Great). Whereas Lutherans might look to Martin Luther as the touchstone of their theology and faith, and the Reformed might look to John Calvin, the Tractarians' devotion to the Fathers inspired a great many Anglicans to look to the early theologians of the Church as the principal exemplars of everything that extended, explored, examined and embodied the witness of the Scriptures, and might thus fit the description 'tradition'. The Tractarians would have recognized their own convictions in the succinct phrase of the contemporary theologian Jaroslav Pelikan, who describes tradition as not the dead faith of the living but the living faith of the dead.[7]

During the Reformation the Protestants accused the Catholics of adding to the faith, while the Catholics accused the Protestants of setting aside historic practice and custom. The

---

7 'Tradition is the living faith of the dead, traditionalism is the dead faith of the living. And, I suppose I should add, it is traditionalism that gives tradition such a bad name. The reformers of every age, whether political or religious or literary, have protested against the tyranny of the dead, and in doing so have called for innovation and insight in place of tradition.' Jaroslav Pelikan, *The Vindication of Tradition: 1983 Jefferson Lecture in the Humanities* (New Haven, CT: Yale University Press, 1984), p. 65.

central Tractarian figure, John Henry Newman, in a highly influential essay in 1845, pointed out that doctrine had never been and could never be unchangeable, but that did not mean it must become corrupt; instead he outlined what he called the 'development' of Christian doctrine, and the concern to keep the Church as much like that of the Fathers as possible.[8] This conviction led him to become a Roman Catholic, not least because such a view of development requires a living authority, which he came to see as the principal rationale for the papacy. Henceforth all Anglican accounts of tradition have been mindful of Newman's journey.

Finally but perhaps most significantly, one more dimension is very evident in the Thirty-Nine Articles which, despite their emphasis on Scripture, are deeply conscious of tradition as a complementary strand of authority. There is a word of caution as to the danger of tradition, as follows:

> it is not lawful for the Church to ordain any thing that is contrary to God's Word written, neither may it so expound one place of Scripture, that it be repugnant to another. Wherefore, although the Church be a witness and a keeper of Holy Writ, yet, as it ought not to decree any thing against the same, so besides the same ought it not to enforce any thing to be believed for necessity of Salvation. (Article XX)

This is a clear warning against the excesses of the Catholic Church as the reformers saw them. But later in the Articles comes a much more positive understanding of tradition:

> It is not necessary that Traditions and Ceremonies be in all places one, or utterly like; for at all times they have been divers, and may be changed according to the diversity of countries, times, and men's manners, so that nothing be ordained against God's Word. Whosoever, through his private judgement, willingly and purposely, doth openly break

---

8 John Henry Newman, *An Essay on Development of Christian Doctrine* (Notre Dame, IN: University of Notre Dame Press, 1989).

the Traditions and Ceremonies of the Church, which be not repugnant to the Word of God, and be ordained and approved by common authority, ought to be rebuked openly, (that others may fear to do the like,) as he that offendeth against the common order of the Church, and hurteth the authority of the Magistrate, and woundeth the consciences of the weak brethren.

Every particular or national Church hath authority to ordain, change, and abolish, Ceremonies or Rites of the Church ordained only by man's authority, so that all things be done to edifying. (Article XXXIV)

Gone is the fierce suspicion of tradition as liable to displace Scripture. In its place is an understanding of traditions and ceremonies in the plural, accentuating the healthy diversity of the Church, which is worthy of the loyalty and adherence of the faithful. And present also is a nuanced appreciation for local discernment, based around the principle set forth in 1 Corinthians 14: that all things be done for the building-up of the Church and the faithful – in short, for 'edifying'.

Whereas the previous two understandings of tradition – the formal and informal teachings and practices from earliest times – have regard for the Church's divine orientation, this understanding is rooted more in the human reality of the Church. Many of the features of Anglican church culture – the clothing, titles and vestments of its clergy, the architecture and furnishings of its ecclesiastical buildings, the liturgical shape and rituals of its church year, the shape and substance of its prayer books, the nature of its theological and ministerial training, the character and order of its councils and synods and general governance – belong amid local custom, practical wisdom and particular circumstance. The irony is that such matters are perhaps more frequently the focus of passionate disagreement among faithful Christians than matters of Scripture and doctrine. (The biggest argument I have ever been called to arbitrate in a congregation was about a stained-glass window.) A more positive perspective on this aspect of tradition that incorporates and blesses local wisdom and custom may appear in regard to prayer. There is no doubt that Scripture offers a host of prayers, including 'The Lord bless you and keep you; the Lord make his face to shine upon you, and be gracious to you; the Lord lift up his countenance upon you, and give you peace' (Num. 6.24–26), and the Lord's Prayer (Matt. 6.9–13; Luke 11.2–4). Yet it also goes without saying, both that such prayers do not exhaust the range of spirituality and that other words and styles of prayer have rightly, through long cherishing, become close to the heart of faith. For example the collect for purity, which begins, 'Almighty God, to whom all hearts are open, all desires known . . .', has an honoured place in Anglican devotion, and indeed the whole body of collects that populate the 1662 Book of Common Prayer and *Common Worship* are widely regarded as one of the truest blessings of Anglican liturgy and among its greatest gifts to the universal Church. It is easy to forget that the rhythm of Morning and Evening Prayer, as set out in the prayer book, is a tradition rooted in the unique practice of the Church of England and thus distinct to Anglicanism – one that is soaked in Scripture but nonetheless has a shape and order that has arisen through custom and circumstance.

Reason

I have referred more than once to the pragmatic, empirical strand in British and American ways of seeing the world. This has several theological grounds. Most especially it lies in the spirit of a conviction about Christ's incarnation. Jesus embraced the contingent, circumstantial detail of embodied human exist-ence – thus paying attention to the particulars of such existence in the world naturally follows as part of a faithful response. More generally this strand draws on a view of creation as the theatre of God's glory, and the healthy aspiration to discern the trace of God's hand in the pattern of the workings and relationships within the universe. But it also looks to the Holy Spirit – for through the Holy Spirit, the God of Jesus Christ becomes known in all manner of places and aspects of life.

Thus to speak of 'reason' as the third aspect of authority – the third dimension of revelation – is to draw attention to a number of ways in which God is made known and humankind responds to God that complement what is expressed through Scripture and tradition. It is also to expect that Scripture and tradition may be rendered in an orderly and comprehensible fashion, which does not simply point to mystery and paradox in the face of the complex and challenging aspects of faith. And it shows a healthy respect for human faculties and investigations that revelation be seen as working with the grain of human wisdom and not always in contradiction to it. Closer attention to the sixth of the Thirty-Nine Articles reveals that this tenor in Anglican theology has been present from the beginning. After maintaining that Holy Scripture contains everything necessary for salvation, this clarification follows: 'so that whatsoever is not read therein, nor may be proved thereby, is not to be required of any man, that it should be believed as an article of the Faith, or be thought requisite or necessary to salvation' (Article VI). Stephen Sykes offers a helpful amplification of what this means for the balance of Scripture, tradition and reason in the Anglican tradition: '[The Article] is not saying that everything which can be read in scripture ought to be believed; but rather that what a plain reader cannot himself find in the text can in no circumstances be required of him as an article of belief.'[9] Here we begin to see what a healthy relationship between Scripture, tradition and reason looks like. Scripture contains everything needed; but not everything in Scripture is needed. Yet everything in Scripture is useful. Tradition distils what in Scripture is needed and employs all in Scripture that is useful, embodying both into forms of life accommodated to building up the body of believers and best equipping it to love and serve the Lord, the neighbour and the whole creation; but tradition should not press upon the Church things contrary to Scripture or give authority to teachings or practices that Scripture does not justify. Reason is a critical friend to Scripture and

---

9 Stephen Sykes, *The Identity of Anglicanism* (New York: Seabury, 1978), p. 90.

tradition, ensuring neither is treated as infallible, holding up a mirror to both, particularly in the face of the kingdom beyond the Church, and seeking to translate both into the language and custom of the day.

Two kinds of distinction within the notion of reason are helpful to bear in mind. One is the difference between deductive and inductive reason. Deductive logic establishes premises, or propositions, which are unambiguous sentences making declarations of fact. It then sets two or more such premises alongside one another and derives a conclusion by accumulating the information disclosed in the respective propositions. For example, two premises might be as follows: miracles are very unusual; Jesus was a person who performed miracles. The conclusion would be: thus Jesus is a very unusual person. One may evaluate deductive logic by assessing whether the premises are respectively true and by checking that the conclusion genuinely arises from the premises. By contrast, inductive logic is a process of inferring conclusions that go beyond the propositions available. Thus unlike conclusions reached through deductive logic, which can be known for certain provided the premises are correct, conclusions reached through inductive logic can never be known for certain. For example, two premises might be as follows: Jesus was raised after lying two nights dead in the tomb; there is no historical record of any event quite like this. The conclusion might be: therefore Jesus' sayings about himself and predictions of his passion and resurrection should be treated with great authority. Almost all faith statements rely on inductive reasoning of this kind. Sceptics, who reject faith as irrational, sometimes imply that deductive logic is the only kind of logic they regard as permissible. However, almost all significant aspects of life require a level of trust, and trust is precisely the quality that inclines a person to rely on the conclusions of inductive reasoning. When Anglicans include 'reason' alongside Scripture and tradition as modes of authority, they are asking that the inductive logic underlying Scripture and tradition be laid bare; the alternative is 'blind faith', which refers to the expectation that one should believe without the inductive process that might lead to belief being made explicit. When reason is contrasted with faith or with revelation, the contrast usually, and unhelpfully, assumes that deductive reason is the only kind of reason in question. The debate between faith and inductive reason is altogether a more fruitful one.

A second distinction is that between theoretical and practical reason. In the simplest terms this is the difference between truth and goodness. Theoretical reason seeks an accurate description of reality; practical reason aspires to an excellent prescription for healthy living. Some philosophers, following Plato, have considered the two almost interchangeable; others, following Aristotle, have regarded them as two almost completely distinct but complementary fields of knowledge. Aristotle described practical reason as concerning matters that can be other; whereas theoretical, or speculative, reason described matters that could not be other – that simply *were*, by necessity.

When challenges are made to Christian faith, it is helpful to make a distinction between challenges made on theoretical grounds and those made on practical grounds. For example, debates between science and religion about such issues as the beginnings of the universe, the origin of species and the plausible historicity of the virgin birth and the resurrection, are questions of theoretical reason. Meanwhile claims that most wars in world history have been caused or fuelled by religious difference or that certain denominations have lost much moral credibility because of the sexual exploitation of vulnerable persons by some placed in positions of trust, are questions of practical reason. To say Anglicanism has been shaped by empirical and pragmatic traditions is to point to the ways Anglican reasoning has tended to be much more practical than theoretical in character. With some exceptions, scientific enquiry has been less troubling to Anglicans than to some others whose identities rest more squarely on confidence in theoretical reasoning. The overall Anglican tendency has been to see practical and theoretical reasoning on a continuum – not ruling out theoretical reasoning as speculative or as contrary to Scripture and tradition, but always seeking principally to establish how the truths of theoretical reason may be translated into the realities of practical existence. Perhaps the most significant way in which this emphasis is expressed is in assuming the primacy of worship as the place in which doctrine (or theoretical reason) is visualized and ethics (or practical reason) is portrayed.

The primacy of practical reason shapes the way Scripture is read and tradition is received. Scripture is not a series of metaphysical (theoretical) claims but is primarily a story of how communities of faith have (practically) responded to the presence and activity of God in their midst. Scripture offers no account of God except in relation to such communities. Tradition is the wisdom of such communities, in the way they have continued best to understand the activity and presence of God among and beyond them and order their lives accordingly. Thus reason is not the (theoretical) seeking of detached first principles as if there had not been hundreds of years of prior experience and reflection on those very things, of which Scripture and tradition are the result; instead it is primarily the practical evaluation of how such wisdom fares in the face of contemporary challenges and scrutiny. There is no such thing as 'reason alone'. All reason arises out of practice and tradition of some kind, including social context, economic status, education, language, cultural norms and much more – and 'Anglican reason' arises out of practices and traditions from within the Church.

But challenge and scrutiny are not idle friends. Reason highlights the sharp edges in Scripture and tradition. Reason names a history of conflict that is evident in Scripture (note the heated debate between Peter and Paul recorded in Acts 15.1–29 and Galatians 2.11–14) and that is present almost ceaselessly in the formation of tradition (note the disaffected believers who did not share the conclusions reached at the Councils of Constantinople and Chalcedon in 381 and 451 respectively). There is nothing inherently unhealthy about conflict: difference and disagreement can become sources of creativity and a refiner's fire for clarity and wisdom. Theoretical reason ensures that Scripture cannot ever simply be taken uncritically for granted, while practical reason ensures tradition will never cease to be tested by the forms of life it prescribes.

A further dimension of reason that has been more prominent in recent times is the increasing attention that has been paid to how the reception of texts and traditions is shaped by the social locations in which they are read and practised. What is sometimes known as the hermeneutic of suspicion – the immediate inclination to mistrust the purpose and design of a text or tradition; the impulse to investigate the power relations behind or hidden in it; and the desire to seek out and uphold the oppressed persons who are taken to be the silent casualties of the legacy – has become commonplace in many parts of the Church at large, particularly in academic circles. Sometimes this means a tendency to regard the past as hopelessly locked into patriarchalism, racism, repression, superstition, intolerance and much else. At other times it becomes an energizing renewal of the Anglican impulse to keep close to the ground and evaluate tradition by how it is received in its particulars.

One final note to reiterate on the subject of authority: never to forget that authority has always been disputed in Anglicanism, and that contemporary debates about it are neither new nor especially distinctive. One helpful and succinct account of authority is provided by a report of a committee of bishops for the 1948 Lambeth Conference.[10] The report notes that 'essentially Anglican' authority is dispersed rather than centralized; its many elements interact through 'mutual support, mutual checking and redressing of errors or exaggerations'; it possesses a 'suppleness and elasticity' that 'releases initiative, trains in fellowship, and evokes a free and willing obedience'. (Note here a heavy emphasis on practical wisdom.) The elements of authority are 'in organic relationship to each other', and the way religious experience is 'ordered, mediated and verified' is likened to 'the discipline of the scientific method'. Scripture describes religious experience; the creeds define it; the ministry

---

10 'The Meaning and Unity of the Anglican Communion', *The Lambeth Conference 1948: The Encyclical Letter from the Bishops; Together with Resolutions and Reports* (London: SPCK, 1948), pp. 84–6, quoted in Sykes, pp. 112–14.

of word and sacrament mediates it; the witness of the saints and the continuing experience of the Holy Spirit (known as the *consensus fidelium*) verifies it; and it is borne out in episcopacy and liturgy. In other words, there is no reason, for Anglicans, that is not, in the end, a form of prayer – a searching, meditating, embodied and Scripture-formed encounter with the ways of God in Christ.

3 The Order of the Faith

Introduction: Holiness

If the first question we considered was, 'What do Anglicans believe?' and the second was, 'On what grounds do they believe it?', the third question, to which this chapter is a response, is, 'What forms of life emerge from this belief?'

Perhaps the central scriptural statement that guides the answer to this question comes from God's words to Moses moments before the giving of the Ten Commandments on Mount Sinai: 'If you obey my voice and keep my covenant, you shall be my treasured possession out of all the peoples. Indeed, the whole earth is mine, but you shall be for me a priestly kingdom and a holy nation' (Exod. 19.5–6). A similar injunction comes from the mouth of Jesus as he utters the Sermon on the Mount: 'Be perfect, therefore, as your heavenly Father is perfect' (Matt. 5.48). Holiness is about two movements – a movement apart, to be distinct, and a movement towards, to be present. Christians are made holy so that they may be a blessing to those they meet and serve.

All three sections in this chapter – worship, ministry and mission – are descriptions of the forms of life that emerge from belief; and all three of these forms of life are attempts to be holy, as God is holy.

Worship is the moment when humans, on behalf of all creation, justified by the grace of Christ, stand before God through the power of the Spirit, in the presence of the angels and surrounded by the communion of saints, seeking to become what God is, holy and eternal, taking their place at the heavenly banquet, and finding their voice in the heavenly choir. Worship is when people, corporately or individually, allow God to make them holy. *Ministry* is when believers open their lives to the Holy Spirit to hear their vocation, take up roles in offering the precious gifts of the Church to believers and adopt lives of humble service in imitation of Christ, seeking to make God's life their own. *Mission* is when disciples seek to discover the holiness of God in the world while bringing the gospel to new people and places, while witnessing to the kingdom of God through care for the neighbour and stranger in body, mind, and spirit, and while opening the structures and institutions of society to the fruits of the Spirit.

Worship

If the faith of Anglicans centres on a conviction, that conviction is that doctrine and ethics, belief and practice, find their meeting place and testing ground in common prayer. If there were one symbol of the convergence of Scripture, tradition and reason, it would be the Book of Common Prayer. In the words of one historian of spirituality in the Church of England:

> To the seventeenth – or indeed nineteenth – century layman the Prayer Book was not a shiny volume to be borrowed from a church shelf on entering and carefully replaced on leaving. It was a beloved and battered personal possession, a lifelong companion and guide, to be carried from church to kitchen, to parlour, to bedside table; equally adaptable for liturgy, personal devotion, and family prayer; the symbol of a domestic spirituality – full homely divinity.[1]

The prayer book has gone through a number of different forms and revisions over the centuries, and both the English 1662 version and the American 1979 version are among the several

---

1 Martin Thornton, 'The Anglican Spiritual Tradition', in Richard Holloway (ed.), *The Anglican Tradition* (Oxford: Mowbray, 1984), p. 74.

volumes that describe themselves confidently, and are known by their users, as The Book of Common Prayer. An important part of what is distinctive about Anglicanism is that it focuses its identity not in an authoritative leader, a declaration of faith or a particular founder or style of governance but in a pattern of prayer. The prayer book is the epitome of the Anglican understanding of tradition: it is a rendering of Scripture, thoughtfully crafted, open to new insights and revisions through the experience of the faithful over time.[2] While the particular language (especially of the 1662 prayer book) has often been the focus of devotion and loyalty, the truer emphasis has been on the pattern itself, which we shall now outline.

The place to begin an understanding of Christian worship is in baptism. Baptism is not usually the beginning of the walk of faith. Faith more often begins in the moment or process of conversion that comes upon an adult believer, and is amplified in the course of instruction (often known as catechesis) that prepares the new disciple for baptism; or it begins in the hearts of the parents of infants who wish that their children know faith first of all as a gift of grace, cherished by familial love, and only secondarily as something to be discovered for themselves. Baptism itself embodies three distinct but overlapping processes in the body and soul of the new believer.

First there is a figurative (or occasionally actual) act of stripping, as the person to be baptized puts behind them all that stands between them and the hands of the merciful God. The imagery is of the Israelites standing on the shore of the Red Sea, with Egypt and the vengeful armies of Pharaoh behind them: the sea will devour all that oppresses, all that causes grief and sorrow and separation between the disciple and God. But the imagery is also that of the returning prodigal son: all the inheritance that was offered to this child of God in creation is poised to be restored; all that is required is for the child to come home, for the damage done by the estrangement has been borne by the ever-loving father and is not counted against him.

---

2 I am grateful to Bill Gregg for drawing my attention to this point.

The stripping of the spirit is a confrontation with God's judgement and mercy; the stripping of the mind is a confrontation with God's desire to free us from slavery; and the stripping of the body is a confrontation with God's power in the face of death.

Then, second, there is the symbolic (or sometimes fully immersing) act of washing. There is the washing of new birth, which embodies Jesus' words to Nicodemus that we must be born of water and the Spirit (John 3.5). As the stripping is a physical enactment of death, this is a bodily enactment of resurrection. There is also the washing of the mind, which echoes the words of Romans 12.2: 'Do not be conformed to this world, but be transformed by the renewing of your minds, so that you may discern what is the will of God.' This moment also echoes the inauguration of Jesus at his own baptism, where the heaven is open to him, the Spirit is upon him and he is wholly embraced by the Father – this is the imagination the new disciple inherits. Yet there is also the washing – or indeed the drowning – of the spirit that recalls the vivid drowning of the oppressors in the Red Sea (Exod. 14–15), and that anticipates God's final judgement on evil. All washing includes this element of drowning – the drowning of that which does not belong in the body.

The third element, more emphasized in recent Anglican liturgies than it had been earlier, is the clothing. Paul speaks of clothing ourselves with 'compassion, kindness, humility, meekness, and patience' (Col. 3.12). This is the activity of the Church in the power of the Spirit. It is marked by activities such as anointing with oil and giving a candle, offering a commissioning prayer and enacting a congregational welcome. This enshrines the bestowing of ministry on each new disciple and is the focal moment of perceiving vocation.

The Thirty-Nine Articles, ever eager to dissipate Roman Catholic accretions, are keen to limit the notion of a sacrament: 'There are two Sacraments ordained of Christ our Lord in the Gospel, that is to say, Baptism, and the Supper of the Lord' (Article XXV). The other five Roman Catholic sacraments – Confirmation, Penance, Orders, Matrimony and Extreme

Unction – are not to be so defined, 'for that they have not any visible sign or ceremony ordained of God'. Anglicans have retained characteristically diverse views on the nature and number of the sacraments, but the caution of the Articles is borne out by the relative reticence in drawing profound significance from the other five sacraments in comparison to the undisputed two. For most Anglicans in the worldwide Communion today, if not in every century before now, the central sacrament, around which liturgical and the rest of life revolves, is the Eucharist.

The Eucharist is centrally a shared meal – almost always a ritualized rather than a full meal. It focuses on the actions of Jesus and the disciples at the Last Supper, where Jesus took, blessed, broke and shared the bread and later took, blessed and shared the wine, declaring that these were his body and blood and that his disciples should henceforth do these things in remembrance of him (Matt. 26.26–29; Mark 14.22–25; Luke 22.15–20; 1 Cor. 11.23–26). These actions recalled the tradition of eating bread and drinking wine alongside eating bitter herbs and a lamb in the context of a Passover meal to celebrate the Jews' escape from slavery and Egypt. Jesus, in this meal and on the cross, becomes the Lamb of God, whose death ensures God passes over human sin, just as the angel of the Lord passed over the houses of the Hebrews that had the blood of the lamb on their doorposts in the days of the Pharaoh. Meanwhile Luke portrays the Last Supper as the seventh meal – seven is the perfect Hebrew number – shared by Jesus in the Gospel narrative: it thus incorporates the significance of all its predecessors, notably the feeding of the five thousand, where Jesus turns scarcity into abundance (Luke 9.12–17). The eighth meal in Luke's account is the supper on the road to Emmaus, where the disciples recognize the risen Lord in the breaking of the bread (Luke 24.30–31): here is the paradigm for the role of the Eucharist in the Church, as a moment in which the disciples continue to discern the presence of the risen Lord. But Jesus' words, 'I will never again drink of the fruit of the vine until that day when I drink it new in the kingdom of God' (Mark

14.25), point to yet a further resonance of this celebration: the great kingdom banquet which is the Gospels' most prominent depiction of everlasting life with God.

Anglicans are concerned with much more than simply recalling the circumstances of the Last Supper. Instead they carry out together an ordered series of actions and words that prepares them to share and receive the sacramental body and blood of Christ, and then to resume their lives, transformed by the body of Christ in all three senses of the term – Christ himself, the Church and the consecrated bread. This ordered series of actions performed by people and clergy together is known as the liturgy. (Liturgy is a generic term for ordered corporate worship, but 'the' liturgy invariably means a traditional form of Eucharistic worship, broadly following the Roman Catholic pattern.) The different orders, or liturgies, for the Eucharist, from Thomas Cranmer's 1549 Prayer Book, through 1662 and later revisions up to contemporary versions, all have slight or significant variations. But across all of them one can discern five movements.

First there is a process of gathering, in which a loose assembly – *ekklesia*, the Greek word for church, originally means assembly – becomes a church; that is, a self-conscious body of Christians seeking in worship to be renewed for mission and in mission to be prepared for worship. Often there is a procession, embodying the Church's status as a pilgrim people, having 'no lasting city', journeying between Pentecost and the last day, 'looking for the city that is to come' (Heb. 13.14). Always there is a greeting, identifying the priest who is to preside over the assembly on that day and naming the presence of God. Sometimes at this point there is a confession of and absolution from sin; by beginning worship in this way Christians are able to enter into the presence of God, free from the burden of their unworthiness. Sometimes there is a song of praise, such as the ancient 'Glory to God in the highest'; and always there is a collect, a formal gathering prayer that literally 'collects' all the disparate intentions of the people.

Second there is the discovery and rediscovery of God's word

in the Scriptures. When the 1662 prayer book was compiled, it was assumed worshippers would already have heard the Old Testament Scripture read at Morning Prayer; thus the readings were simply a Gospel passage preceded by a text from elsewhere in the New Testament. Today, in many parts of the Anglican Communion, Holy Communion is the central act of worship and thus the Old Testament is read alongside a psalm and the two New Testament Scriptures. The Gospel, since it records the words of Jesus, is usually given special honour by being heard standing. The sermon follows, and is a proclamation of the piercing word of the Scripture in the context of today's Church and world: it is perhaps the most evident moment in the Church's life when Scripture, tradition and reason meet.

Third there is the response to the hearing of God's word. This usually includes a recitation of the Nicene Creed, the most explicit statement of the Church's tradition of faith; it almost always involves the articulation of prayers of intercession (sometimes called prayers of the people), calling on God to rend the heavens and visit again struggling and suffering people, in the style described in the Scriptures; it incorporates a confession and absolution, if not conducted earlier; and very commonly an exchange of signs of peace, recalling Jesus' words, 'When you are offering your gift at the altar, if you remember that your brother or sister has something against you, leave your gift there before the altar and go; first be reconciled to your brother or sister, and then come and offer your gift' (Matt. 5.23–24).

Fourth, there is the sharing of food. Gifts of bread, wine and sometimes money are brought to the altar, and this symbolizes the best of human efforts, rather like the five loaves and two fishes that were all that the disciples could muster at the feeding of the five thousand (Matt. 14.15–21; Mark 6.35–44; Luke 9.12–17; John 6.5–14). The priest calls on the people to lift their hearts and to adopt an attitude of thanksgiving. In the prayer that follows, the priest recalls the story of God's unfolding purpose through creation and covenant before taking the bread and wine, invoking the power of the Holy Spirit on them and on the congregation, pronouncing Jesus' words at the Last Supper and then calling on God, through the fruitfulness of the sacrament, to renew the Church and all creation with justice and mercy. (The sequence of the prayer varies according to custom.) The Lord's Prayer is said and the bread is broken before the sharing takes place.

Fifth, and sometimes quite briefly, there is a sending out for mission and ministry. A final thanksgiving is offered, and the congregation is blessed and dismissed – commissioned to celebrate the Eucharist they find in the world, to transform what is not a cause of thanksgiving into one, and to bring back to the altar the following week all that has been good and all that is in need of transformation.

What exactly takes place when the priest recalls Jesus' words (known as the words of institution) and invokes the transforming power of the Holy Spirit? This was the focus of much debate during the Reformation and has remained a divisive question since. There are broadly four established understandings. The characteristic Roman Catholic view is that the bread and wine continue to look like bread and wine but their true nature has been changed into Jesus' body and blood. Thus the worshipper truly is partaking of Christ's body. The characteristic Lutheran view is that the bread and wine remain bread and wine but that Christ, who is divine, enters believers at the moment they receive the bread and wine. The characteristic Calvinist perspective is that Christ, being fully human, cannot be in more than one place at once, and is in heaven, but that the bread and wine constitute a promise that the Holy Spirit will give to the disciple Christ and his 'benefits' (forgiveness of sins and everlasting life) when the Eucharist is shared. The characteristic Zwinglian belief is that the Christian already has Christ, and that the words and actions at the altar are a reminder for Christians of the blessings they already possess.

The typical Anglican congregation will, when canvassed, reveal a range of views across this spectrum. Anglican doctrine has never identified itself with one of them. It is simply assumed that during the prayer of thanksgiving the Holy Spirit acts upon the elements and during the receiving of communion acts within the believer. Most prayers of thanksgiving are carefully balanced to incorporate language that echoes and honours all four traditions. Thus when the priest says, 'This is my body . . . This is my blood', it sounds like the Roman Catholic view is being portrayed. Yet when the priest prays that the bread and wine 'may be for us the body and blood of our Lord Jesus Christ', the words 'for us' are a clear gesture towards the Lutheran understanding. Most prayers likewise include the language of 'promise', pointing to the Calvinist perspective, and 'memorial', suggesting the Zwinglian view. This ambiguity, yet relative harmony, among the four understandings is the most prominent of many doctrinal and ecclesial compromises made by Anglicans. In practice the congregation's broad perspective is indicated by a number of signs that are seldom visible in the written liturgy. Thus if the table is called an 'altar' and the clergy wear the white alb and richly coloured stole and chasuble associated with Roman Catholic worship, and if the architecture places the events in a lofty and exalted place, these are gestures towards a more Catholic view of the proceedings at the table. If instead the term 'holy table' is used, fewer if any formal vestments are worn and the event is known as the Lord's Supper, these are gestures encouraging a more Zwinglian view. But these are matters on which, following the tradition of Queen Elizabeth I, the Church in general has no desire to make windows into its members' souls.[3]

While the two central sacraments significantly shape Anglican worship, they do not dominate it. Three other dimensions contribute to its general character. Thomas Cranmer, Archbishop of Canterbury (1533–56), took five of the seven Benedictine daily offices (or regular prayers) and crafted Morning Prayer or Matins (from the services of Matins, Lauds and Prime), and Evening Prayer or Evensong (from the services of Vespers and Compline). These acts of worship bookend the day for

---

3 Elizabeth used this phrase to say that she did not expect conformity and unanimity – simply loyalty to her, to the nation and to the Church across a broad spectrum of theological opinion.

Anglicans. They are centered on the reading of Scripture and the recitation of the psalms, and have a cherished place for scriptural and traditional canticles, the Apostles' Creed, brief responsorial prayers and memorable collects. Over the centuries an enormous body of music has been composed for these services, and the psalm chants and canticle settings have become an important part of the Anglican contribution to the universal Church. In the twentieth and twenty-first centuries the Eucharist has tended to displace these offices as the most prominent congregational act of Sunday gathering. Yet for a great many Anglicans, particularly those whose confidence in their own participation in the ministry and mission of the Church is tentative but whose pursuit of holiness and the search for the mystery of God is genuine, Morning and Evening Prayer remain key dimensions of corporate worship. They embody the significance of prayer to doctrine and the centrality of Scripture to worship. In the Church of England at least, they also represent the honoured place of the sincere seeker and person of hesitant conviction within the notion of the Church.

Just as the regular rhythm of Morning and Evening Prayer orders the daily shape of time, so the liturgical calendar orders the yearly sense of season. There is a time for celebration – notably Christmas and Easter and also Ascension and Pentecost; and there is a time for introspection and penitence – in Lent and Advent. There are saints' days to honour the Church's heritage and see the unity of the faithful living and departed. And in-between there are periods of 'ordinary time' to fill out the texture and breadth of Christian experience.

A further dimension of worship lies in the occasional offices, notably weddings and funerals. In keeping with the tradition of expressing faith in prayer, rather than in formal declarations, the understanding of marriage is to be found in the words said at the beginning of the marriage service. Here Anglicans find three purposes of marriage: mutual joy; companionship, especially in adversity; and when and if the gift is given, the procreation of children and their nurture in the faith. Marriage is seen as established in creation, blessed by the first miracle of Jesus at Cana in Galilee, and as offering a sign of the union between Christ and the Church. The Church does not marry people; they marry one another: the Church simply witnesses, celebrates, seeks to meet God in Scripture and prays for and with the couple. In blessing a marriage the Church seeks for the couple to be made holy. Thus in a way somewhat similar to ordination, the couple is set apart and enjoined to adopt a form of common life in order the better to be present in ministry and mission to Church and world.

Likewise funerals and memorial services are not occasions when the Church does something 'to' the deceased person. They are occasions for considering a person's life in the light of eternity and for commending them to God's grace; for giving thanks and proclaiming resurrection faith in the face of sadness, grief and many other responses to loss; for offering support and strength to mourners while gently bringing the congregation face to face with their own mortality and degree of preparedness for it – all in the context of worshipping the living God. In almost every case the deceased's life showed and taught, intentionally or unintentionally, something of the character of God, and the act of worship is a balance between what God gave in the gift of this person's life and what God gave in the gift of Christ and continues to give in the gift of the Holy Spirit. Thus such acts of worship are a prayer that the deceased's life may be safe with God and may, in its entirety, be a blessing to God's people.

All of these and many other dimensions of corporate worship both fertilize and are fertilized by the soil of personal prayer. Such prayer may follow a set liturgy, such as the form of Morning or Evening Prayer; it may be devotional, focusing on a passage of Scripture, a commentary or meditative reading, an icon or the consecrated bread; it may be contemplative, beyond word or image into the heart of God; it may be charismatic, open to pictures or words that speak prophetically to the self or to others; it may be purposeful, eagerly interceding for a particular concern over a long period of time or repeating a short form of words over and over; it may be systematic, methodically keeping lists of causes or persons and raising each, day by day; or it may follow the rhythm of a journey to work, a daily walk with a dog or the chore of ironing. Everything in Anglican theology assumes and furnishes an understanding of personal prayer. Having a formal prayer book offers a model for personal devotion, and keeping a regular rhythm of Sunday worship offers a pattern for personal faith. But there is no assumption that such personal faith should be expressed formally – only that in joy and in sorrow, in wonder and in need, at morning, noon and night, at the dining table and in the quiet of the bedroom, the believer should turn to God in penitence, praise, thanksgiving and expectation.

Ministry

Ministry is a fruit of baptism. As soon as new disciples are incorporated into the body of Christ in baptism, ministry is bestowed upon them. All ministry is Christ's ministry, so all ministry derives from being a member of Christ's body.

The Church uses the terms ministry and mission in overlapping ways. Mission tends to refer to what members of the Church do in relation to those who do not gather to worship – whether sharing faith in evangelism, sharing resources in humanitarian efforts or building institutions and working towards transformed social structures. Meanwhile ministry tends to refer to the ways the Church orders its common life – educating its children, catechizing those new to faith, conducting its worship, managing its finances and buildings, sustaining its governance, training its clergy, overseeing its staff, offering pastoral care of the faithful. The overlaps are considerable: offering regular worship, for example, is part of the Church's mission but is clearly an aspect of common life; likewise most Churches offer pastoral care not just to members but to all who seek it. The simplest but not always the most accurate way to configure the interconnection of the two terms is that *ministry* is disciples' self-conscious participation in the Church's *mission*.

Thus there are a host of activities that rightly come under the designation of ministry. The greater awareness of the connection of ministry to baptism has led in recent years within the Anglican Communion to a growing sense of the ministry of the whole body of Christ, often crystallized in terms such as 'every member ministry'. Some of these ministries, such as youth work, children's work, preaching and leading worship on the part of lay people as well as Eucharistic ministry to the housebound, have come to involve particular training and licensing. Many other vital roles, such as financial management and the raising of funds, are not licensed but are nonetheless integral to the flourishing of the Church.

One thing that all of these activities have in common is that they are forms of the worship of God and the service of others to which the believer may expect to sense a call. Vocation is a place in the soul of the believer where creation and redemption meet; that is to say, it is a place where the manner and urgency and grace with which God redeems the world in Christ through the Holy Spirit resonates with the character and disposition and qualities of the created person. Vocation does not simply affirm the innate gifts of the disciple, it bestows gifts upon the disciple. Those called to ministry are not necessarily those whose gifts are most evident or brilliant, but God clothes those who are called with gifts sufficient to their task. Such vocation is seldom if ever simply an individual response to an individual word from God: vocation emerges through communal discernment and is a reflection not just on personal potential but on fruits witnessed by others.

Among myriad ministries one has a particular place – not a higher place but nonetheless a unique one. That place is designated by the term ordination. Some practices of the Church – notably baptism, preaching, the pronunciation of the forgiveness of sins, blessing and the celebration of the Eucharist – are so fundamental to the life of the body that persons are set apart to care about and specialize in carrying them out faithfully and thoughtfully. There are many lay ministries associated with these foundational activities, such as reading Scripture, catechizing new believers and assisting with the distribution of communion. But ordained ministry signals a distinct trust – dwelling in call, competence, training and prayerful pursuit – that these central formative practices are being administered well. From time to time that trust is jeopardized, for example when a member of the clergy turns out to be living a life that falls painfully short of the community's expectations of conscience and conduct. But the validity of these core practices does not depend on the character of the person who leads them: the Holy Spirit offers treasure even through clay jars (2 Cor. 4.7). In Anglicanism the symbol of that trust is often the clerical collar. The collar communicates that this is a person whose theological formation, gifts in ministry, understanding of Scripture and tradition, rhythm of prayer and transparent character make them ready, at any moment, to encounter God in and with God's people, in joy, mundanity or despair.

After the Reformation the Church of England – and the Anglican Communion subsequently – retained the threefold order of ministry: bishop, priest and deacon. This is a significant feature of Anglican claims to be both catholic and apostolic. The role of the deacon is variously understood in different denominations. In the Church of England it is a special ministry of servanthood in which the particular objects of service are 'the poor and weak, the sick and lonely and those who are oppressed and powerless'. Special attention is given, for deacons, to making 'the love of Christ known through word and example', and showing that in serving such people 'you are serving Christ himself'.[4] The tradition is that those to be ordained priest are first ordained deacon. They become used to ordination and the community become used to them, for a period of months or more, until the time comes for them to be ordained priest. This tradition has the disadvantage that diaconal ministry is widely seen as little more than a transitional state, which is an impoverishment of a rich ministry that goes back to the Acts of the Apostles. Some few, however, remain deacons permanently,

---

4 http://www.churchofengland.org/prayer-worship/worship/texts/ordinal/deacons.aspx.

affirming the servant-heartedness central to all ministry but particularly represented by this role.

The priest is an intermediary between God and the people. Martin Luther and others among the great reformers insisted that the people *as a whole* were an intermediary between God and the world – hence Luther's emphasis on the term 'the priesthood of all believers'. This term originates in Israel's designation in Exodus 19 as a 'priestly kingdom' – that is, a collective priest between God and the nations and indeed the whole created world. It does not mean that every believer is a priest – Israel itself had representative priests, from the lineage of Aaron. These priests offered sacrifice in the temple in Jerusalem, burnt incense and in general mediated between God and Israel. Many Protestant denominations have preferred the term 'pastor' (shepherd) or 'minister' (servant), often remaining suspicious of the term 'priest' because it is associated with sacrifice (and also of the term 'altar' for the same reason). In practice the term 'priest' for Anglicans is not centrally about the notion of a sacrifice taking place at the altar. It is about the role of an intermediary between God and the people.

Is such an intermediary necessary? Christ is after all the 'one mediator between God and humankind' (1 Tim. 2.5). Anglicans do not believe an intermediary is strictly *necessary*; they may commune with God in Christ through the Holy Spirit anytime, anywhere – they do not need someone to intervene on their behalf. But they also believe priesthood is nonetheless a gracious gift of God to the Church, one that focuses, refines, embodies and unifies the people's prayers and becomes a channel of profound blessings.

Four roles assemble around the person of the priest. First, a priest represents the people to God. This is expressed liturgically in the praying of the collect, where the priest gathers together the diverse and diffuse prayers of the congregation and collects them into one prayer that concludes the gathering of the people before God and focuses all their attention on the source of their creation and salvation. It is sometimes done at the prayers of the people, where the priest not only brings the unresolved, unexplained and unhealed to God on behalf of the people but also models how the people are to stand before and address God. It is sometimes done in the prayer after communion and in the collect for purity, where well-honed words are carefully expressed to shape the way the worshippers perceive their role in worship and beyond. But in recent years many if not all these parts of the liturgy have come to be said jointly by priest and congregation or, in some cases, by a single lay person. And so attention focuses even more on the one part the priest alone says: the prayer over the bread and wine known as the Great Thanksgiving. Beyond the Sunday liturgy this role is perhaps most evident when the priest prays the office (Morning and Evening Prayer), ideally in the parish church: he or she is then with God with the people on his or her heart (to use a term associated with Michael Ramsey, Archbishop of Canterbury 1961–74). Whenever the priest reassures a parishioner, 'You'll be in my prayers', this is the relationship that is being identified.

Second, a priest represents God to the people. When sins are forgiven a declaration is made. This is speaking to the people for God. A sermon is preached, making the words of the scriptural text sing in the congregation's ears and dance in their hearts. This again is speaking for God. An announcement is made that the peace the people are about to share is the peace of Christ. The bread is broken and the words bring the past significance and power of Christ's death into the present reality of sharing his risen body. A blessing is given to seal the grace of God in the hearts of believers, and again these words are spoken for God to the people. And because the priest speaks such a word in the liturgy, people look to the priest for similar words at other times. When parents say, 'How can God let my child get leukaemia?', when a farmer says, 'What d'you think God is up to with this run of weather?' or when a mother says, 'Is my boy marrying a young woman of another faith a terrible thing?', the expectation is that the priest will have something to say, something from a deep storehouse of wisdom, something to show for all the time spent in the presence of God, something true to the heritage of faith but fresh for the circumstances of the moment. These conversations are the heart of ministry.

These are the two core roles: speaking to God for the people and to the people for God. But churches are human institutions too, and the priest invariably takes on two additional, ancillary roles.

One is the role one might describe as the chair. The chair's role is not to lead but to ensure leadership emerges; not to decide but to ensure a decision is taken at the right time by the right people in the right way; not to dominate but to ensure that no one and nothing dominates besides the commitment to building up the church. Without a chair, a group doesn't know how to start, what to talk about, who should speak, how to make a decision and how to finish. The other most significant ancillary role is the role of the facilitator. This role is more playful, more like a chef composing a recipe with the ingredients that happen to be available, more given to improvisation, lighter on its feet, adept at employing humour, not averse to using charm, enticing people into a dance. While the chair is always focused on the final purpose of the assembly and how best and most directly to get there, the facilitator is much more focused on the gifts each person is bringing and what thing of beauty might be made with them that is uniquely possible with *this* cocktail of people and unimaginable without the vital permission given each person to bring forward their gifts and let them work and play together.

The ministry that most distinctively unites Anglican Churches is that of the bishop. There is no assumption of unanimity in the Church: on the contrary, the Church has been, from the earliest times, in ongoing debate about the sources of its authority and the nature of its task. The bishop therefore does not seek or impose uniformity but inspires loyalty from clergy and lay people and, through word and action, clarifies the mission of the Church in general and the diocese in particular. In the service of the ordination of a bishop in the Church of England, the archbishop declares, 'Bishops are ordained to be shepherds of Christ's flock and guardians of the faith of the apostles, proclaiming the gospel of God's kingdom and leading his people in mission.' These words follow:

> They are to baptize and confirm, nurturing God's people in the life of the Spirit and leading them in the way of holiness. They are to discern and foster the gifts of the Spirit in all who follow Christ, commissioning them to minister in his name . . . With the Shepherd's love, they are to be merciful, but with firmness; to minister discipline, but with compassion. They are to have a special care for the poor, the outcast and those who are in need . . . Following the example of the prophets and the teaching of the apostles, they are to proclaim the gospel boldly, confront injustice and work for righteousness and peace in all the world.[5]

All bishops trace a line of authority reaching, in direct succession, back to the earliest apostles. Their role is to guard the faith, unity and discipline of the Church. While special missionary contexts might require unusual forms of proclamation, ministry or witness, the bishop is the guardian and teacher of the faith of the apostles. Likewise while circumstances and travails may help to explain why prominent persons among the clergy or elsewhere have struggled to uphold the standards expected of them, and profound cultural influences and temptations – and even a sense of call or gospel urgency – may have pushed whole congregations into peremptory or graceless action, the role of the bishop is to guard the discipline of the Church while exhibiting simplicity, firmness and kindness. The presence of sin among the flock is always a disappointment but should never be a surprise; the bishop models to the faithful what discipline and restoration look like when exercised among individuals or larger bodies of people.

More than anyone else, the bishop is the spokesperson for the Church in two key areas: to the watching world and to the

---

5 http://www.churchofengland.org/prayer-worship/worship/texts/ordinal/bishops.aspx.

wider Church within the Anglican Communion and beyond. Bishops join with other bishops in leading churches across their own province and around the world. They are the physical, embodied representatives of their dioceses. This also makes them suitable figures to interact with representatives of other faiths. And it makes them recognizable persons of authority, wisdom and integrity to address the secular world, locally and more broadly, on issues of common concern, bringing a characteristic Anglican concern for the common good.

Mission

What are the Church's hopes for the world and what role does it perceive itself to have in bringing these hopes about? These are the questions of the Church's mission, which is really an aspect of God's mission. In the life of the Trinity, God the Father sends the Son, and God the Father and the Son send the Spirit. Then there is a third 'sending': the Father, the Son and the Holy Spirit send the Church into the world. The sending of Church to world may be considered under the broad headings of past, present and future.

In relation to the past the Church seeks to understand, cherish, conform its life to and – most significantly – make known the good news of what God has done in Christ. This is the work of evangelism. There is nothing inherently coercive, imperialistic or disrespectful about evangelism. Evangelism is seeking to present the good news of God, specifically of God's determination never to be except to be with us, and the outworking of that faithfulness in the incarnation, ministry, death and resurrection of Jesus and the sending of the Holy Spirit. Any presentation of this message in a pressurizing or manipulative manner misrepresents and thus diminishes the gospel it purports to proclaim. Evangelism is properly conducted on many levels: individually, through personal and relational invitation, challenge and testimony; congregationally, through corporate initiatives to share faith through grand or humble schemes; and intercongregationally, through larger-scale programmes and para-church ministries.

There is also, in relation to the past, the important work of memory. There is so much to be cherished and tenderly unearthed, so much wisdom to be celebrated, witness to be admired, sacrifice to be honoured and example to be imitated. This is perhaps especially significant in relation to those whose lives were, at the time, considered of little or no account, who because of their gender, race, class, disability, youth or other social circumstances were not given in their day the honour due – and yet can now be seen or discovered to have left a legacy that speaks of goodness, truth and beauty. This is indeed the work of mission, to search for lost coins in the household of history, coins that, gathered together, may furnish the present and future with limitless gold.

At the same time memory is not just about cherishing. It is often about challenging. Many wrongs have been done: some well-known, others never told; some in Christ's name, others ones whose fruits are felt to the present moment; others still whose injustice is perpetuated, practised and even inflated today. Wrongs of the past cannot be erased but they should not be ignored or denied. The work of mission includes the commission to translate evil – the pervasive, insidious disease of sin that passes itself off as good – into individual sins that can be named, truthfully narrated, repented of, forgiven and in due course healed. This process is of tremendous significance even when the perpetrators and victims themselves are long gone, for the recalling of history, its nurturing in bitterness and resentment, its transformation through truth-telling and repentance, and its healing through long struggle and profound grace, is at the heart of the gospel.

Turning to the present, the most important aspect of mission is the modelling of what God makes possible in the quality of the common life of local congregations and fellowships. If there is no practice of forgiveness, no witness of eternal life, no fruits of the Spirit, no love of God, neighbour and self, no joy in worship, no faith, hope or love in local community and neighbourhood, there is nothing for the persuasive voice of evangelism or the plaintive cry for justice to point to. There is a role for calling for other houses to be put in order but it requires the Church to put its own house in order – a crucial aspect of mission. The ability to live in peace, even with those with whom you agree, requires grace. But the ability to make a community of faith that is more than the sum of its constituent parts, from those with whom you don't instinctively agree, requires the Holy Spirit and is a profound witness to the God who, in Christ, has broken down the dividing wall of hostility.

Committed to such humble reconciliation within its own body, the Church seeks to foster and celebrate the life of the kingdom of God wherever it flourishes and wherever it is most noticeably endangered. The irony of the kingdom of God is that its flourishing and peril can be found in the same place – just as they were on Calvary. Much of the joy of mission is simply to share it with those who have the same reason 'for the hope that is in you' (1 Pet. 3.15). Often initiatives for mission and unity overlap because there are few things that build up unity more successfully than a shared sense and practice of mission. The forging and establishing of more profound unity with Christians from different geographical, race and class locations is an integral aspect of mission.

Jeremiah's words to the Jewish exiles in Babylon, 'Seek the welfare of the city where I have sent you into exile, and pray to the Lord on its behalf, for in its welfare you will find your welfare' (Jer. 29.7), inspire Christians to partner with those of all faiths and none around projects and programmes that enhance the good of their neighbourhoods and societies. Such partnerships are goods in themselves, and not a means to any further end. Nonetheless they build trust, help congregations know their neighbourhoods better and show the humanity of the gospel in its concern for the mundane and ordinary aspects of created life. By participating in the mission of God, Christians seek not simply to do good but more to make the ordinary good and the good holy. One of the most important aspects of this ministry is peacemaking. War and armed conflict inflict death and damage upon whole populations, and the cause of peace, while of particular concern to Christians whose Lord blessed the peacemakers (Matt. 5.9) and taught his disciples to love their enemies (Matt. 5.44; Luke 6.27), concerns the welfare of all people.

In many places, through oppression, misfortune, hardship or disaster, Christians, those of other faiths, and those of no faith experience poverty and other profound forms of social alienation. Here again the mission of the Church is to form partnerships with those of different backgrounds, based around enabling disadvantaged people to find their own way to forms of social healing and stability. There are significant drawbacks around any form of support that never results in face-to-face contact, relies heavily on monetary gifts to third-party agencies and assumes what is required is expertise and material resources; for such intervention can underline as well as alleviate poverty in the long and short term. If the heart of the Christian faith is that God resolves to be *with* us and only works *for* us on occasions when such ministry is needed in order to restore such companionship, any form of mission that assumes the priority of *for* over *with* can only be provisional and suitable, for example, in emergency conditions. The key partners in alleviating poverty are socially disadvantaged people themselves. The parable of the Good Samaritan (Luke 10.25–37) is not simply a mandate to attend to distress wherever and in whomever we might come upon it, however inconvenient; it is a call to recognize ourselves in the person in the ditch and realize that the person whom God sends to save us may be one whom everything in us is reluctant to see as our benefactor. Meanwhile in the parable of the last judgement Jesus points to the hungry, the thirsty, the stranger, the naked, the sick and the prisoner as bearing his own identity, and insists that on the last day he will say, 'Just as you did it to one of the least of these who are members of my family, you did it to me' (Matt. 21.31–46). This inspires Christians to expect the activity of the Spirit to be most vividly manifested in the most troubling of circumstances – and seldom in those most conscious of the righteousness of their own actions.

The enjoyment of the common life of the Church, the experience of right relations in shared mission and fellowship, the sense of partnership in local and regional social initiatives and the compassionate desire to be with the poor in their distress leads to two further aspects of mission in the present tense. One is the development and practice of expert skills in key areas of human well-being. Among those, two have stood out from New Testament times to the present day: education and health. Education is not simply the fostering of faith and the cherishing of the wisdom of the ages; it is the passing-on to the poor of their most dynamic route out of poverty. The large-scale mission projects of Western Christians in the nineteenth and early twentieth centuries, which sought to introduce whole populations in Africa and elsewhere to the Christian faith, were dominated by schools and hospitals. Christians are involved in education and health because, of the places of transformation in which the Spirit is deeply invested and frequently tangible, these are the most pervasive. A vocation to be a teacher or a healthcare professional has long been regarded as among the highest callings for a lay Christian; and monastic communities have likewise been associated with these aspects of patient, skilled ministry more than with any other aspect of mission.

The final aspect of present-focused mission arises out of reflection on the *causes* of the social ills that so much of Christian mission seeks to address. What leads people to slide into poverty? What keeps them there when everything in them longs to escape? What brings about huge disparities of wealth, miserable living conditions, constant vulnerability to violence and crime, imbalance in treatment by the law, undemocratic voting regulations, oppressive working relations, shortage of food, chronic health problems and high infant mortality? Such concerns, and many others, are often grouped together under the term injustice. A significant dimension of Christian mission is the identifying of places and perpetrators of injustice, the naming of structures of oppression, the articulation of the cries of the suffering and the campaigning, lobbying and deal-making involved in seeking executively or legislatively to put things right. This is an area of compromise, not perfectionism – of pragmatic progress, not principled obstruction; the purpose is to set people free not simply spiritually and eternally but materially and bodily and presently. This form of mission often leads people into protest and subversion, but it can equally well lead to institution-building and legal training.

There is also a future aspect to mission. It has a particular and a general dimension. The particular dimension is that the Church is called to portray in its present life the future shape of God's coming kingdom. This means relationships of forgiveness and reconciliation but also, and most poignantly, actively seeking to be present among and offer hospitality to those closest to Jesus' heart – the socially excluded by difference, by disadvantage, by oppression or by their own sin. Jesus' ministry portrayed the ingathering of the exiles; so must the Church's life be.

The general dimension, more pertinent in this age than ever before in the Church's history, is the forging of peace not just between humankind and God nor even between humans one with another, but especially between humanity and the wider creation. It is not that, should human beings destroy the world this would thwart God's plans or bring creation to an end; God is capable of restoring the world whoever's was the hand that destroyed it. Instead Christians demonstrate their hope for the magnitude and scale of the new heavens and the new earth by the way they cherish the world in the time between the times. Mission is not saving the world; it is gratefully and joyfully seeking to live and share the life of the Spirit made possible by the way God in Christ has already saved the world.

4 The Character of the Faith

Introduction: Incarnation

Incarnation tells the story of what happens when the full disclosure of humanity to God meets the full disclosure of God to humanity. It is not a smooth ride, as the Gospels make clear. There have been theologians and preachers ever since who have maintained that the interaction of God and humanity is, or ought to be, a straightforward matter for both parties. This has seldom proved to be the case. Thus incarnation, perhaps the theological term most associated with Anglicans, names the inseparability of divine and human destiny – but at the same time incorporates the fragility and failure and sharp edges as well as the noble aspirations of mission through the centuries. Jesus is born in obscurity, yesterday and today; he faces danger and finds nurture, yesterday and today; he teaches, heals and faces conflict, yesterday and today; he is betrayed and tried and crucified, yesterday and today; he is raised from the tomb and breathes his Holy Spirit on his disciples, yesterday and today.

All this we see in the three overlapping stories that make up this chapter, which are told in different ways. The account of the Englishness of Anglicanism attempts to distil its character less into an arbitrary and constructed notion of Englishness than into certain key decisions, events and movements that continue to shape the Church of England today. The account of American dreams shows how wrong it is to see Anglicanism through English eyes only or even primarily: few if any Churches of the Anglican Communion have been less determined by the imperial imagination than The Episcopal Church, and thus few are as well placed to exhibit how Anglicanism develops its own dynamics in relation to local culture, local history, local faith and global partners, just as much as from English impulses. The story of global Anglicanism offered here is inevitably incomplete in scope, not just in detail: key areas such as the Caribbean, Latin America, the Middle East and the Far East are overlooked altogether. I have sought to give an account that emphasizes the role of local evangelists and does not play into the assumption that the growth of Churches always followed the contours of the British Empire and the initiative of daring British missionary entrepreneurs.[1] One consequence of this is that my account tries to acknowledge honestly the sense of lament that must accompany a truthful telling of the story of much Christian missionary activity, notwithstanding the brave individuals who went against the grain and spoke up for a deep engagement with and respect for local cultures and leadership. It is not for nothing that a leading British theologian seeks for the Church of England to become a 'pioneeringly honest ex-oppressor church'.[2] It is not for nothing also that this account concludes with Ireland, one land that as much as any other has reason to wonder whether Anglican witness in its midst has, overall, constituted a blessing.

English Legacies

I shall attempt to characterize the distinctive features of English Anglicanism by identifying a number of key dates and elucidating their significance.

The first date is 664. In that year the Synod of Whitby – near York, on the north-east coast – convened representatives of the Celtic and Roman traditions. The Celts had brought Christi-

---

1 In this I have deliberately followed the ethos and work of Kevin Ward, *A History of Global Anglicanism* (Cambridge; New York: Cambridge University Press, 2006), on which this account is closely based.

2 Andrew Shanks, 'Honesty', in Samuel Wells and Sarah Coakley (eds), *Praying for England* (London; New York: Continuum, 2008), pp. 125–46.

anity from Ireland via the west-coast Scottish island of Iona and the north-east Northumbrian island of Lindisfarne. The Romans traced their heritage to Pope Gregory the Great and his sending of Augustine of Canterbury in 597 to convert the English. The pretext for the synod was to come to a common mind on the manner of establishing the date of Easter. The victory of the Roman party marks a symbolic, decisive and largely permanent shift in English Christianity from Celtic to Roman dominance. Put differently, England was and is part of Europe, culturally and religiously, and not primarily part of an island – or group of islands – unto itself; and yet it is not as wedded to Europe as most of its continental neighbours. The Church of England is the same. It is part of Catholic Christianity, part of the Reformation heritage; and yet it has significant local character, Celtic and otherwise, that makes it unique.

A second date is 1075, when Pope Gregory VII overhauled the parish system throughout Europe. Theodore of Tarsus (Archbishop of Canterbury 668–90) largely adopted the existing Anglo-Saxon township structure, wherein minster churches in the towns served the countryside around, until landowners oversaw the construction of smaller churches whose parishes largely coincided with the boundaries of the gentry's estates. Each parish, at least in theory, had its own priest. The role of the parish priest was renewed by Dunstan (Archbishop of Canterbury 959–88), who enhanced both the clergy's education and their role in promoting the well-being of all who resided in their parish. Pope Gregory VII's reforms brought the English parish system into line with that which covered most of Europe. It is hard to overestimate the significance of the parish for the imagination of English Anglicanism. The parish embodies the Church of England's commitment to the flourishing of every resident of the land, and demonstrates – in the way the priest shares the life of the people – that God cares about what they care about, thereby embodying God's love for humanity in minute particulars and the everyday rhythms of life. This is how the Church of England expresses its care for place and for the poor; this is its essential ministry of presence and its orientation to seek God in the ordinary and abiding, the fragile, the contingent and the tragic. The economics of being so tied to the landed classes has sometimes meant that the Church has come adrift from the poor and been slow to respond to urbanization both materially and imaginatively; these are the weaknesses of its strengths.

A third date is 1559. The English Reformation was about governance and faith but it was not always about both. Thus for King Henry VIII, England was an empire that had no need to be subject to the pope, being rather directly under God's own decree – as was legislated in 1534. Henry had no desire to innovate in doctrine or alter the Catholic faith. By contrast his chief minister, Thomas Cromwell, was inspired by Martin Luther and sought to introduce the new Protestant perspective under the guise of reforming the Church's governance. Likewise Thomas Cranmer, Archbishop of Canterbury (1532–56), set about revising the Church's liturgy in line with Reformed notions of priesthood and sacraments, as represented in his prayer books of 1549 and 1552. For Queen Mary, who ruled from 1553–8, and who was a Roman Catholic, governance and faith lay together, and both lay in obedience to Rome; but on her death Queen Elizabeth restored English governance, while seeking a balance between Catholic order and Reformed faith – such a compromise constituted the Elizabethan Settlement of 1559. Henceforth a wide diversity of theological convictions have found their authority in this story of origins, and the Church of England has never been well placed to take the high ground as regards freedom from state interference. But the Settlement made English Anglicanism an almost unique *via media* between Catholic and Reformed faith, and this is part of its inherent character.

The next date, 1662, is the only one that has become almost a proper name, because it indicates the publication of the Book of Common Prayer that has been used in most Churches in the Anglican Communion at least until the 1920s and in many cases to this day. The English Civil War (1642–51) and the time of the Commonwealth and Protectorate (1651–60) brought to the surface several groups, notably Presbyterians, Independents (later Congregationalists) and Baptists, as well as more radical groups such as the Quakers. The Restoration, in which Charles II was brought to the throne in 1660, restored also a Church and liturgy much more in line with the 1552 prayer book, setting aside Reformed order and worship.

The Book of Common Prayer characterizes English Anglicanism at least as much as the parish system. It shows that the Church's identity lies in prayer rather than doctrinal structure or declaration, and it affirms that public prayer is the definitive form of prayer. Such prayer is 'common' – in other words, not primarily for the 'religious' but held in common by all. The assumption is also that such prayer is founded on the written word rather than the extempore spirit, being inscribed on the heart by habit and repetition.

Yet 1689 represents the limits of the vision of 1662. When King James II looked certain to restore Catholicism in England he was, in 1688, deposed by a united Protestant front. While 1660 had shown that England would not become wholly Protestant, 1688 had shown England would not become Catholic either. But the dissenting Protestants were not going to go away, and in the Act of Toleration of 1689 they were allowed to worship legally in parallel to the Anglican parish system. (In 1828 they were given full rights – a move extended to Catholics in 1829.) The notion of the Church of England as the Church for all the English thus failed; and the Church of England became, in reality if not in its own imagination, one denomination among others. The Oxford Movement, an engine of Catholic renewal in the Church of England, began when it became clear that the nation's Church – governed by Parliament – was now in its doctrine and order being overseen partly by dissenters and Catholics. It is at this point that the identity of Anglicanism – a term first used around this time – became identified less with Englishness and more with specific liturgical, doctrinal and historical commitments, such as more frequent Communion and the introduction of vestments in worship, almost all of which were (and are) deeply contested.

The date 1867 marks a more significant reason why Anglicanism could no longer simply be identified with Englishness. Anglicanism had become a loose federation of Churches most of which had strong links to the English Reformation. These included The Episcopal Church in the USA, the Scottish Episcopal Church, which departed from the Presbyterian Church of Scotland in 1582, and the Churches shaped significantly by British colonial expansion, including Canada, India, Australia and the West Indies. All of these began to take on an identity influenced but not dominated by the Church of England. One key date in this process is 1799, which marked the founding of the Church Missionary Society (CMS). The Church of England failed to incorporate the Evangelical Revival of the eighteenth century, most notably Methodism, within its structures; but one fruit was the impetus that English politician William Wilberforce among others gave to overseas missions. Thus CMS began with three goals: abolition of the slave trade; social reform at home; world evangelization. Its great leader from 1841 to 1872, Henry Venn, coined the 'three-self principle' for overseas Churches: self-government; self-propagation; self-finance. In 1867 the Archbishop of Canterbury, Charles Longley, convened the first Lambeth Conference of Anglican bishops, and 76 of the 144 bishops attended.[3] Thirteen further conferences, around every ten years, have been called since. A distinct style of leadership has emerged: the Archbishop of Canterbury convenes the conferences but has no official authority beyond England; the conference resolutions are not decrees but guides to future action; the provinces are tied together by bonds of affection rather than obligation.

In a very different vein, 1870 brought the Education Act of Prime Minister William Gladstone's reforming Liberal government. Prior to this, education had been largely in the hands of the Churches, especially the Church of England. Henceforth the government funded schools where they did not previously

---

3 Of the 76 bishops who attended, 18 were from England, 5 from Ireland, 6 from Scotland, 28 were 'colonial and missionary' bishops, and 19 were from the United States (http://www.lambethconference.org/resolutions/).

exist, in a decisive move towards universal education. Education still remains, to a degree unthinkable in the Anglican Communion outside Britain, profoundly influenced by the Church, with, for example, a daily act of worship prescribed by law – if not always honoured in practice – in every school. There still remains, in many parts of England, an assumption that if children are to discover the Christian faith they may be expected to do so in school – a remote and alien thought in places such as the USA, where such is more or less forbidden by the Constitution. There are nearly 7,000 state-funded faith schools in England today, most of them overseen by the Church of England.[4] Education has long been the principal frontier of the Church of England's mission.

The twentieth century marks the era when active church participation became a minority pursuit. Three dates perhaps summarize this period. The first is 1941. In that year William Temple, Archbishop of Canterbury 1942–4 (along with George Bell and Michael Ramsey, the most remarkable church figure of the century) convened the Malvern Conference, attended by 400 priests and lay people with speakers including T. S. Eliot and Dorothy L. Sayers. It was the darkest hour of the war but Temple was already envisaging a country fit for victorious soldiers to return to. The Labour government of 1945–51, with its wide-ranging welfare reforms, owed a great deal in its vision and imagination to Temple and the conversations he ignited. Temple more than anyone else embodied the Church of England's commitment to social ethics and its willingness to seek the common good while closely concerned for the poor. The *Faith in the City* report of 1985, calling attention to the plight of deprived inner- and outer-urban areas, lies squarely in this tradition. But the welfare reforms marked the takeover by the state of many of the social roles hitherto performed by the Church – and thus, while building up the kingdom of God, hastened the Church's decline.

The next date encompassing English legacies is 1964. John Robinson, the Bishop of Woolwich in south London, published

---

4 http://www.guardian.co.uk/education/2001/nov/14/schools.uk2.

Honest to God, an attempt to popularize some liberal post-war theological movements in an effort to make Christianity comprehensible to a secular age. It sold a million copies in ten years. While it promoted the fresh air of honest theology, it was more memorable for the traditional affirmations it undermined than for the newer convictions it advocated. It epitomized a wind of change sweeping Church and society; and one statistic that characterizes that change is that Church of England ordinations fell from 636 in 1963 to 273 in 1976 – a precipitous decline.[5] Believing is clearly not identical to or even fundamentally characteristic of belonging. Nonetheless the '*Honest to God* debate' identifies a secular confidence, a sense that the world was comprehensible without recourse to faith, or at least Church, that remains highly significant in English culture and that found its high watermark in the 1960s.

An important date is 1967. In this year a thousand Church of England evangelicals, led by John Stott, the long-time rector of All Souls, Langham Place in London, met at Keele in Staffordshire. Prior to Keele, in the words of one prominent evangelical scholar, evangelicals in England were associated with 'archaic theology, spiritual conceit, ecclesiastical isolationism, social unconcern, pessimism about the world and the Church, an old-fashioned lifestyle, and a cultural philistinism'.[6] After Keele, evangelicals entered conversations about poverty, liturgy, ecumenism and perhaps most of all the Eucharist, with an energy not seen for generations. The result is that today, having entered and invigorated the structures and moved out of the shadows, evangelicals make up the most vibrant, engaged and populous dimension of the newly ordained, the regular worshippers and the financial supporters of the Church of England.

Women were finally admitted to the priesthood in 1994. They had been formally admitted as deaconesses since 1869, as readers since 1969, and as deacons since 1987. Yet in order to pass this legislation through General Synod (the Church of

---

5 Adrian Hastings, *A History of English Christianity 1920–2000* (London: SCM Press, 2001), p. 552.

6 James Packer, quoted in Hastings, p. 553.

England's legislative body), a system of alternative episcopal oversight was established, recognizing the 'two integrities' of those who did and those who did not endorse women as priests. This inaugurated a period of considerable complexity, more acutely felt in some dioceses than others. It also set a precedent that was bound to be capitalized upon when the General Synod initiated a draft law allowing women bishops in 2010; and it ushered in an era of multiple ecclesial realities that started to become even more elaborate once the global controversy over the ordination of those living openly homosexual lifestyles began in earnest. The Church of England has prided itself on being one large tent; it is not clear whether it can continue so to describe itself as that tent becomes increasingly divided into sections with fewer flaps linking the respective sections together.

American Dreams

Christians often assume that they know what Judaism is: Christianity with the New Testament removed. Thus they invariably ignore the enormously significant developments in Judaism since the time of Christ, and have a hugely impoverished understanding of Judaism. A similar dynamic tends to be at work in the English Anglican's view of The Episcopal Church. The tendency is to assume that The Episcopal Church is simply the Church of England without the monarch at its head and bishops in the House of Lords. But in reality it has, from its very beginnings, differed in form and conviction from the Church of England.

One distinctive feature of The Episcopal Church has been the significant role played by the laity at every stage in its development. There was no bishop until the consecration of Samuel Seabury by bishops of the Scottish Episcopal Church in 1784. Thus for well over 150 years, since the first missionary clergy were sent to Virginia, there were congregations dependent on a mixture of overseas funding, lay stewardship and, in

North and South Carolina, Maryland, Virginia, Georgia and New York City, funding from the government in accord with being the established Church. Nonetheless many of these congregations had no clergy for lengthy periods, and much of the provision of worship came about through lay initiative. The overseas funding largely derived from the London-based Society for the Propagation of the Gospel in Foreign Parts. (When the War of Independence began in 1776, the stronger parishes tended to side with the patriots whereas the weaker parishes, more dependent on English support, tended to be loyalists.[7]) The seventeenth- and eighteenth-century Church was primarily a lay movement – and this deep history of lay leadership equipped it well for the turbulent times after independence, and is still significant today.

The American Revolution constituted a nervous breakdown for much of the Church and, once the era had passed and the new arrangements were in place, American Episcopalianism faced a struggle not only to form a new identity but to secure its very survival. While it may be difficult to perceive it as such from a twenty-first-century perspective, the Revolutionary War seemed to some contemporaries in the Church of England to be uncomfortably reminiscent of the English Civil War 130 years earlier. Puritan refugees from seventeenth-century Anglican domination in England had shaped the culture of New England, and even though several signatories of the Declaration of Independence were in fact Anglican laymen, many Anglicans in America and England saw the revolution as a Puritan revolt. And this perception is not entirely an eighteenth-century relic: the notion that the monarchy and the excessive authority of bishops constitute forms of oppression of which Americans still do well to be wary, is a view that is still heard in Episcopal Church circles to this day.

The post-Revolutionary disestablishment of religion shook the Church of England in the former colonies to its core. Quickly, the newly birthed Protestant Episcopal Church had to

---

7 See David Hein and Gardiner H. Shattuck Jr, *The Episcopalians* (Westport, CT: Praeger, 2004), p. 38.

find new ways of financing itself. It also had to adjust to a resident episcopacy – having never had its own bishops before. And
it had to compete in a religious marketplace. The emphasis on
lay leadership served the Church well in this new context. The
role of the laity is born out in the governance of The Episcopal
Church. The first General Convention of The Episcopal Church
took place in 1785. Its constitution, like the 1781 US Constitution, drew on an underlying Presbyterian ethos, and sought to
balance interests that might find themselves in conflict, reflecting republican assumptions. Originally there was one house of
deputies, made up of clergy and laity; in due course a house of
bishops was added, yet with no conclusive power of veto. The
Episcopal Church tends to have a confidence in its constitutional
arrangements comparable to the confidence of the nation as a
whole in the serviceability, sufficiency, adaptability and unique
virtues of its own constitution. There is, accordingly, no question that the date 1791 marks a profound difference between
the identity of The Episcopal Church and that of the Church
of England. The First Amendment to the Constitution, passed
in that year, begins with the words, 'Congress shall make no
law respecting an establishment of religion, or prohibiting the
free exercise thereof.' Thus there is no governmental role in
advancing or inhibiting religious practice. In more recent years
this has been understood as not just a federal proviso but one
restricting all levels of government.

It might be thought that the Civil War of 1861–5 would be
at least as devastating for The Episcopal Church as the Revolutionary War had been. A precedent was set when the dioceses
within the Confederacy created their own, separate Protestant
Episcopal Church in the Confederate States of America. (The
Episcopal bishops of Louisiana and Georgia were two of the
largest slaveholders in the country.[8]) The division of the state
required, it seemed, the division of the Church. The relative
silence of church leaders in the midst of the crisis may seem
disturbing today: the Boston preacher and hymn-writer Phillips
Brooks commented that Episcopalians seemed unsure 'whether

---

8 Hein and Shattuck, p. 77.

there was a war going on or not, and whether if there was it would be safe for them to say so'.[9] Yet this quietism in the pulpit contributed to an atmosphere whereby reconciliation of the two Churches followed not much more than six months after the conclusion of such a devastating and divisive war. Nonetheless it was only eight years later, in 1873, that the Church split again – this time over ritualism. Some more evangelical members found the Catholic liturgical tendencies, arising from the Oxford Movement in England in the 1830s and 1840s, unacceptable, and established the Reformed Episcopal Church, which as late as 2009 reported over 13,000 members.

A particular characteristic of The Episcopal Church is that while it tends to be associated – by non-members – with an upper-middle class cultural ethos, it nonetheless sees itself as closely concerned with issues of social justice. This paradox has long been the case. Before the Civil War, African Americans had been members of The Episcopal Church in significant numbers, albeit in many, perhaps most cases as slaves rather than by their own choice. After the war The Episcopal Church engaged in a long and substantive debate about appropriate ways to do ministry with and for the freed slaves, many of whom were church members. Unlike, for example, the Methodists, The Episcopal Church never formally split along race lines; yet it expended considerable efforts to create separate arrangements and institutions that in the end kept African Americans subordinate – notably the founding of a black-only seminary at Petersburg, Virginia, in 1878 and the consecration of two black bishops, Edward Demby and Henry Delany, to work specifically among African Americans. (It was the emergence of the 'Jim Crow' Laws, especially around the time of the First World War, that gave segregation the roots and form that make it such a painful memory today.) From the 1950s such provisions began to unravel: for example, a resolution at the 1952 General Convention forbade seminaries or colleges from using race as a pretext for excluding certain students, and in 1954 the diocese of South Carolina welcomed three black parishes

9 Quoted in Hein and Shattuck, p. 77.

into its convention. The lawyer Pauli Murray, later to become the first African American woman ordained in The Episcopal Church, played a major role in the lead-up to the landmark 1954 *Brown vs Board of Education* decision on school segregation.

The role of Native Americans in The Episcopal Church has seldom received the same level of either contrition or attention. This is a story with many signs of hope, with significant presence and ministry in Oklahoma, Milwaukee and Minneapolis among other places.[10]

The Episcopal Church's sense of its own unique role in society was expressed in two late-nineteenth-century initiatives that have significant parallels with contemporary developments in England and abiding resonances to this day. The first was the annual gathering known as the Church Congress that first met in 1874 and considered the major issues of the day. These congresses offered a forum for the sharing of a wide range of theological opinions, one factor that contributed to The Episcopal Church's being able to navigate controversies, such as the science–religion debate over evolution, more equably than some other denominations. They also established The Episcopal Church's concern for the transformation taking place as the United States became an industrial society – concerns known as the 'social gospel' movement and articulated extensively by the Episcopalian laywoman Vida Dutton Scudder. This attention also led to the setting apart by the Bishop of Maryland of five women in 1857 as the Church's first deaconesses (an order officially recognized in 1889), and to the prevalence of social outreach ministries among downtown churches. Here the prominence of the incarnation, so much associated with late-Victorian English Anglicanism, found deep roots in Episcopal Church soil. A second wave of incarnational ministry, in which affluent Episcopalians set out to live in socially disadvantaged neighbourhoods, came about in a number of north-eastern cities in the 1950s.

---

10 Ward, pp. 62–3.

The second development was the growth of the national church ideal. Christianity was becoming increasingly associated with American identity and perceived, along with democratic civilization and education, as part of the unique gift of the United States to the world. The building of the National Cathedral (an Episcopal foundation) in Washington, DC, which began in 1907 (and ended in 1990), is the most striking symbol of the conviction that The Episcopal Church was America's natural national Church. Another aspect of this conviction was the assertion of the Chicago-Lambeth Quadrilateral (see Chapter 2), first proposed by William Reed Huntingdon in 1870 and adopted by the Episcopal House of Bishops at the 1886 General Convention in Chicago.[11] This sense of confidence was matched by the Church's tripling in size from nearly 350,000 to over one million members from 1880 to 1920 (rising to 3.3 million by 1960).[12] Meanwhile commitment and success in spearheading ecumenical relationships resulted in the Bishop of the Philippines, Charles Brent, being invited to chair the first World Conference on Faith and Order at Lausanne, Switzerland, in 1927. However, attempts in the 1930s and 1940s to unite with the Presbyterian Church in the USA failed. The same conviction about having a broad responsibility without being an established Church was behind the role played by The Episcopal Church in laying down institutional foundations for the Anglican Communion – notably the founding of the Anglican Consultative Council in 1969. Those who have decried The Episcopal Church in recent years for stretching the bonds of communion have perhaps at times forgotten how much The Episcopal Church did to forge them in the first place.

The Episcopal Church found itself profoundly divided by the turbulent social movements of the 1960s. It is arguable that the Church remains divided between those who continue to see these movements – in relation to race, war, gender and,

---

11 Huntingdon saw one of The Episcopal Church's key advantages as a truly national Church lying in the fact that, unlike Roman Catholicism, it was ethnically pure. See Hein and Shattuck, p. 89.

12 Hein and Shattuck, pp. 112, 119.

by extension, sexuality – as definitive, and those who do not. The contrast is simply expressed in the succession of presiding bishops. Jim Hines, presiding bishop from 1965 to 1974, self-consciously sought to locate Episcopalians on the side of the dispossessed and oppressed peoples of the nation. His successor, John Allin, presiding bishop from 1974 to 1986, while he considered himself a liberal by Mississippi standards,[13] opposed the ordination of women and had an altogether different set of concerns from his predecessor. These differences were reflected in The Episcopal Church more broadly. For some, an unjust law was no law at all; for others, civil disobedience was a polite name for lawlessness. For some, Christ came to save the world and political action was all of a piece with worship, pastoral care and evangelism; for others, politics was a dangerous distraction from the true work of the Church.

The circumstances of the first ordination of women to the priesthood are especially significant for the self-understanding of The Episcopal Church. Proposals had narrowly failed at the General Conventions of 1970 and 1973; those who saw the question as one of civil rights were eager to stage some kind of direct action to bring the Church to its senses. Thus it was that two retired bishops, together with one who had recently resigned from his diocesan position, acting contrary to the will of the local bishop, ordained eleven women before a congregation of 2,000 in Philadelphia in July 1974. A year later another retired bishop ordained four more women to the priesthood in Washington, DC. The House of Bishops expressed profound misgivings. It seemed to many that procedure, authority and discipline were in open conflict with love and justice. In 1976 ordination at all three levels was opened to women; by 1979 there were almost 300 women in ordained ministry; the first woman bishop was ordained in 1989.

Given the increasingly polarized character of The Episcopal Church (one way in which the Church has reflected

---

13 'Bishop John Maury Allin, 77, Former Leader of Episcopal Church, Dies', Nichole M. Christian, *New York Times*, March 8, 1998; at http://query.nytimes.com/gst/fullpage.html?res=980CEFDF1430F93BA35750C0A96E958260.

the dynamics within American society more generally), it is remarkable and admirable how broad a consensus formed and continues around its 1979 Book of Common Prayer. In the Church of England it has long been common for Anglo-Catholics to incorporate elements of the Roman missal and for Anglican evangelicals to take pride in making their worship 'non-liturgical' – often perceiving doing so as making worship more 'seeker-friendly' and thus serviceable for evangelism. By contrast in The Episcopal Church, the use of a written and shared liturgy is a significant and striking point of unity across the theological spectrum. Within the 1979 Prayer Book one line is cited perhaps more than any other in current debates of faith and order. It is the final question of the eight parts of the Baptismal Covenant: 'Will you strive for justice and peace among all people, and respect the dignity of every human being?'[14] For some in the contemporary Episcopal Church these words have attained the force of Martin Luther's famous words, 'Here I stand; I can do no other.'

To understand the contemporary controversy over homosexuality it is essential to recognize that the debate arose in a context where The Episcopal Church had already long (at least since the 1960s) been committed to a trajectory that defined itself by what the Baptismal Covenant calls 'respect for the dignity of every human being'. As one observer puts it, 'The Anglican church worldwide can no more contrive permanently to marginalize homosexual people or remove them from its fellowship than it could continue to accept slavery, the inferiority of women, or the natural superiority of European civilization.'[15] Meanwhile there had always been vocal elements in The Episcopal Church that believed either that such 'social justice' causes were a distraction from the central call to worship, discipleship and evangelism or, additionally, that because acceptance of homosexual lifestyles seemed to contravene Scripture, the ordination of homosexual priests and

---

14 The Protestant Episcopal Church in the USA, *The Book of Common Prayer* (Church Hymnal Corporation and Seabury Press, 1979), p. 305.
15 Ward, p. 315.

bishops constituted an unacceptable doctrinal departure. After the 1998 Lambeth Conference it became clear that the wider Anglican Communion was going to regard American judgements on these matters as having global ramifications; and that elements within The Episcopal Church opposed to the by now almost inevitable movement towards the formal recognition of the legitimacy of homosexual lifestyles were looking to secure the oversight of bishops from the global South – moves that cut them off from local episcopal structures. Thus the ordination of a partnered gay man, Gene Robinson, as Bishop of New Hampshire in 2003, was not a watershed moment but one step in a long-term realignment of those with diverging but previously not irreconcilable understandings of faith and mission in the United States and beyond.

Global Dimensions

The global Anglican Communion defies generalization. While I very much hope that the vast majority of its 80 million members worldwide would gladly subscribe to the description of the faith I have offered in the first three parts of this book, there is not a great deal else that would be shared by almost every member of the global Church. Only 16 of the 38 provinces use the term 'Anglican' in their Church's name. The Scots, Americans, Filipinos and Sudanese, for example, use the term 'Episcopal', while the term 'The Church of . . .' is widely used, for example in England, Ireland, Pakistan, Nigeria and Uganda. And there are other distinctive names such as 'The Church in Wales' and 'The Anglican Episcopal Church in Japan'. Most provinces have developed their own indigenous liturgies. It is no longer the case that every Church sends its bishops to the decennial Lambeth Conference. In what follows I can therefore only aspire to offer some flavours of this considerable diversity.[16]

There can be no doubt that the heartland of the Anglican Communion today lies in Africa. Britain abolished the slave

---

16 Most of this section is drawn from Ward.

trade in 1807, but British participation in the transportation of around 10–15 million persons from West Africa across the Atlantic over the preceding 300 years was not, and is not, a legacy easily dispelled. Many former slaves – known as recaptives, their descendants as Creoles – returned in the early 1800s to West Africa, after which their relations with indigenous tribes remained complex. For a great number of them Christianity seemed to be the source of their freedom, and Anglican practices took root, especially in Sierra Leone. One freed slave was Samuel Ajayi Crowther, who was born in 1806 in what is now northern Nigeria, enslaved in 1821 but soon released by the British. He was baptized in 1826, ordained in 1843, translated the Bible into Yoruba and was ordained bishop in 1864. Crowther was a key figure in blending the local culture with the practices of Christianity. The white missionaries, however, struggled to entrust church leadership to local people (there was not another African-born diocesan bishop until the 1950s), even though the missionary work was largely conducted by local pastors and evangelists. While the size of the churches, particularly in Nigeria, increased dramatically, there remained two unresolved tensions: the ability of Anglicanism to adapt itself to local customs and accommodate local notions of marriage, healing, spiritual forces and so on; and the encounter with the equally rapidly expanding presence of Islam. The Church of Nigeria (Anglican Communion) today is vibrant: it has an estimated 20 million members, around 100 dioceses, a vigorous campaign of evangelism in the largely Muslim north, a strong attachment to the 1662 Book of Common Prayer, significant charismatic influences and a decidedly conservative stance on issues of sexuality and women's ministry.

While Anglicanism came later to East than to West Africa, East Africa has become the second major area of its flourishing today. Uganda has around nine million Anglicans, Tanzania and Kenya a further four million between them. The persecution of Christians by the Kabaka from 1885 to 1887, in which many local Anglicans and Roman Catholics, together with the Bishop of Eastern Equatorial Africa, James Hannington, were executed, still lives long in the Ugandan Church's memory. The first Ugandans were ordained in 1893, and Alfred Tucker became the first Bishop of Uganda in 1897. In 1913 Bishop Tucker Theological College – today Uganda Christian University – was founded in Mukono. The success of Anglican evangelism in Uganda relied upon the power of arms to subdue the Kabaka and keep the Muslims in check. British missionaries prioritized the conversion of the cultural elites and the education of the next generations of those elites; the poorer classes tended to become Catholics, although the Anglican bush schools were widespread and effective. A major step towards freeing the Anglican Church in Uganda – known now simply as 'Church of Uganda' – from colonial constraints was the East African revival, which began in Rwanda in 1935 and deeply affected Uganda, Tanganyika – as Tanzania was then known – and Kenya. It had a radical gospel of equality between black and white, strong anti-paganism, strict monogamy and piercing honesty: in all it was a reassertion of a new communal African identity, and its influence has only been surpassed in recent years by the widespread Pentecostal movement. Uganda experienced a second era of martyrdom during the rule of Idi Amin, including the killing of Archbishop Janani Luwum in 1977. Both before and after Amin's regime, Anglicans have been closely, perhaps too closely, associated with the Uganda People's Congress; nonetheless Yoweri Museveni, president since 1986, has defused much sectarian tension. The long-running insurgency of the so-called Lord's Resistance Army in the north of the country has meanwhile brought the Churches to a greater sense of common cause. The Anglican Church of Uganda has been a leader in responding to the HIV/AIDS crisis in East Africa. It has also had a role in the contemporary controversies in The Episcopal Church in the USA: since it regards itself as in full communion with the Anglican Church in North America, it is deeply in tension with The Episcopal Church.

The Episcopal Church of the Sudan claims five million members. It traces its history independently of the East African provinces, being more closely related to the Churches of the

Middle East. The key figure was Archibald Shaw, who adapted the Christian faith to the culture of the nomadic Dinka people in southern Sudan and brought to ordination the first Sudanese bishop, Daniel Deng Atong, in 1955. The East Africa revival was influential in many parts of southern Sudan, and the Zande people took more readily to the faith than had the Dinka. Independence in 1956 sparked an almost continuous civil war between the Arab north and the Christian and animist south, which only concluded in 2005, independence for the south following in 2011. Much suffering resulted from the relentless war: Sudan epitomizes the suffering Church within the Anglican Communion.

It is impossible to tell the story of the Anglican Church of Southern Africa (which has two and a half million members in South Africa and perhaps another million in nearby states) without recognizing the complexity of the colonial and apartheid eras. The first Bishop of Cape Town, Robert Gray, was appointed in 1848, not long after the end of slavery ten years earlier. He established the principle of a Church that included all races – a principle considerably ahead of its time, and often breached but nonetheless significant. He appointed John Colenso as Bishop of Natal in 1852. Colenso learned the Zulu language and painstakingly sought to redefine doctrines of sin and justification to adapt to local circumstances and wisdom. He also embraced the new 'historical-critical method' of biblical criticism, which was considered a radical move at the time. Bishop Gray disagreed on all counts and tried Colenso as a heretic in 1863. Colenso claimed Gray had no jurisdiction over him and won his case, remaining bishop until his death in 1883 and advocating the Zulu cause – although Gray's party became dominant in the Church thereafter. (The widespread disquiet about the case was a significant pretext for the calling of the first Lambeth Conference in 1867.) In the lead-up to and aftermath of the 1899–1902 Boer War, concern about how Anglicans related to the Afrikaner population obscured sustained attention to the injustice being perpetuated towards the non-white communities, particularly in relation to land and voting rights.

From 1948, the victory of the National Party regularized and formalized segregation under the policies of apartheid. Alan Paton was an early white Anglican who voiced theological objections in the 1940s; Ambrose Reeves and Trevor Huddleston were others whose voices came to be heard in the 1950s; and Gonville ffrench-Beytagh and Hannah Stanton continued the prophetic stance in the 1960s. The government continued to dismiss the Anglican Church as the continuation of outdated British colonialism, and the Anglican Church in general failed to make the gestures and statements that would prove this was not so. The key representative of a very different kind of Anglicanism was Steve Biko, a Xhosa medical student who founded the Black Consciousness Movement and was involved in the World Student Christian Federation. He was beaten to death in police custody in 1977. Desmond Tutu was the second key figure. He became General Secretary of the South African Council of Churches in 1978, Archbishop of Cape Town in 1986 and visible representative of the spirit of the Kairos Document, which asserted a prophetic theology in place of church (aka Anglo) and state (aka Afrikaner) theology. Tutu's role in the Truth and Reconciliation Commission that followed the end of apartheid is perhaps the most significant political contribution of an Anglican cleric anywhere in the world in the contemporary era. Nonetheless South African Anglicanism has, a little like The Episcopal Church, become so politically oriented that many have wondered if it still has a place for them; meanwhile many Africans still see it as less indigenous than, for example, the Pentecostal Churches.

The Church of South India (CSI) and the Church of North India (CNI) represent two major ecumenical endeavours. In India, unlike in Africa, the Church of England sought to serve the needs of the European population and not to disturb the religious ecology of the native peoples. Gradually in the 1800s evangelical missionary work was permitted and dioceses were created; but by the 1900s Indian nationalist sentiment was becoming a concern. Thus only one Indian, Samuel Azariah, was made a bishop in the whole of the colonial era. In general the missionary approach was to convert the elites and not to dwell too extensively with the poorer classes. Negotiations to form a union of the Anglican, Methodist and Reformed Churches in South India began in 1919 and culminated in the formation of the Church of South India in 1947, a month after Indian independence. Many English Anglicans, including T. S. Eliot, were deeply troubled about the infringements on episcopal order that seemed inevitable in an ecumenical polity, and the CSI had to wait until 1998 for its full recognition in the Anglican Communion; but it has thrived because of rather than in spite of the extent of its ecclesial diversity. While outstanding missionary bishops included Lesslie Newbigin, the Church has from the start been very largely Indian in character and leadership. The Churches in North India were weaker, and their ecclesial structure was disrupted by the creation of first Pakistan in 1947 and then Bangladesh in 1971. Nonetheless the Church of North India came into being in 1970, including, unlike its southern counterpart, Lutherans, Baptists and Disciples of Christ. The two Indian Churches have a combined membership of over five million.

Oceania remains one of the most numerically significant Anglican regions. Over 70 per cent of Oceanic dwellers are Christian, and Anglicans make up around 18 per cent of the population.[17] The Anglican Church of Australia has around 3.7 million members, making it larger than The Episcopal Church in the United States. Two features of its contemporary and historical life stand out. One is how uncomfortable has been its relative difficulty in finding a flourishing place for Aboriginals in its life. Vernacular culture was largely ignored or eradicated: citizenship was only extended to Aboriginals in 1967, and the fiction that the land was unoccupied before the first settlement was established in 1788 remained official history until the late twentieth century.[18] James Noble was the first Aboriginal to be ordained deacon in 1925, but it was not until the 1970s that there were further ordinations. Arthur Malcolm

17 Ward, p. 274.
18 Ward, p. 282.

became the first Aboriginal bishop in 1985. In 1988, Archbishop John Grindrod apologized to the Aboriginal and Torres Strait Islanders people for hurts done to them. The other feature is the way patterns of Irish and Scottish immigration have carried with them antagonisms and commitments in Australia: most obviously, Sydney diocese has been known throughout the Anglican Communion, for at least the last 50 years, for its profoundly conservative and outspoken Reformed stance, theologically and socially – a position deriving in great part from Irish Protestant legacies. This stance has given Sydney diocese more formidable resources to withstand the rapid secularization of Australia and to adapt to charismatic influences.

By contrast the relationship of the Anglican Church in Aotearoa, New Zealand and Polynesia with its indigenous Maori people has been somewhat less tortured – as its name indicates. The initial mission was to the Maori population (rather than to the settlers), and a treaty safeguarding the Maori was signed in 1840. This treaty, while inadequately framed and implemented, has nonetheless proved a boon to the Maori people. The first Maori bishop, F. A. Bennett, was appointed in 1928. Today the Church, numbering half a million, maintains the right of every member to choose the cultural stream – Aotearoan (Maori), Pakeha (white) or Polynesian – in which they wish to express their faith. The primacy is accordingly shared between three archbishops, and the 1989 Prayer Book is a self-conscious celebration of diversity.

Addressing diversity and a complex historical legacy is likewise the key to understanding the Anglican Church in Canada, which numbers around two million – around half of whom are in Ontario. As in Australia, Canadian Anglicanism took on a strong Irish Protestant character from the nineteenth century, and maintained a prominent role for lay women in mission. First Nations peoples had often been seen as key military and economic allies in the revolutionary period, but later came to be politically marginalized. However, Anglican missions were fruitful, and today 25 per cent of Canadian Indians and 85 per cent of Inuit people are Anglican – comprising 10 per cent of the Anglican Church in Canada's membership as a whole. But the systematic deculturation that took place in the residential schools continues to overshadow this history, and the offering of adequate compensation threatens to bankrupt more than one Canadian diocese, beginning with Cariboo in British Columbia in 2001. Anglicanism has not taken deep root among Francophone Canadians, although the more recent influx of Haitian and Congolese Anglicans has altered this historic tendency somewhat. Canada has led the Anglican Communion in moves towards same-sex blessings, with less (internally) divisive results than corresponding developments in the USA.

One repeated phenomenon in considering global efforts from the Church Missionary Society (CMS) and Society for the Propagation of the Gospel (SPG)[19] and other English-based organizations has been the prominence of Irish and Scots missionaries.[20] While small in number, the Scottish Episcopal Church (50,000), the Church of Ireland (350,000) and the Church in Wales (75,000) have each in different ways modelled a non-established Anglicanism.

In Wales the Reformation affirmed Welsh identity by bringing about the translation of the Prayer Book in 1567 and the Bible in 1588. Much later the leaders of the Welsh Great Awakening (1735–98) were in many cases Anglicans. However, as in England the established Church was unable or unwilling to keep the surge of faith within its structures. As late as 1905 the Church in Wales was still the largest denomination in the principality, and even after disestablishment in 1922, and perhaps uniquely among Anglican Churches, it retains a non-established mission to all who dwell in the country.

The 1707 Union with England affirmed Presbyterianism as the established Church of Scotland; and because of its association with Jacobite pretenders to the throne (the last of whom died in 1792), Scottish Episcopalians remained largely in the

19 In 1965 the SPG merged with Universities' Mission to Central Africa to become the United Society for the Propagation of the Gospel (USPG).

20 'The CMS came to occupy a much more central role in Church of Ireland life [in the nineteenth century] than it ever did in the Church of England' (Ward, p. 27).

shadows, indeed sometimes persecuted, until the nineteenth century. Thereafter the Scottish Episcopal Church retained a certain social cachet: Presbyterians were said to think 'that the Episcopal Church is an English exotic brought in by the laird [lord] with his background of an English public school, or by the laird's English wife, and supported mainly by people who hope the laird will ask them to dinner'[21] – an impression not hindered by the invariable appointment of Englishmen as bishops until the later twentieth century. The assertion of a more authentic Scottish tradition, generally Anglo-Catholic in character, and always more deeply rooted in the north-east, was assisted by the publication of Scottish prayer books in 1929 and 1982.

The political manipulation that has often lingered within Anglicanism has perhaps surfaced in Ireland more often and with greater ill-effect than in any other land. Despite the establishment of Trinity College, Dublin in 1591 to train men for the cause, the Protestant faith did not take hold in Ireland; it did not help that evangelists assumed that converts should speak English. In the late sixteenth and early seventeenth centuries English and Scottish Protestants were planted in Ulster and Munster, and 40 per cent of the land was transferred to their ownership. One outcome was the 1641 rebellion, during which many Protestants were massacred in Ulster. Protestant ascendancy took hold decisively after the defeat of James II by William of Orange at the Battle of the Boyne in 1690. The Act of Union (1801) and the Evangelical revival encouraged the (Anglican) Church of Ireland in the false hope of making Ireland Protestant; but disestablishment, which came in 1867, was a more sober statement that religion, like land, needed to be detached from the Irish question as systematically and urgently as possible. After partition in 1922, the Orange Order continued to harbour hopes for Protestant ascendancy in the North, and the Church of Ireland remained, in many places, deeply invested in securing Protestant dominance by various means, although its leadership has been increasingly associated

---

21 Agnes Muir MacKenzie, 1943, quoted in Ward, p. 30.

with peacemaking. In the Republic of Ireland, the Church of Ireland continues to be linked to more affluent, influential parts of society, but is much more comfortable with a minority social context.

Conclusion

What does the story of English, American and global Anglicanism and Episcopalianism add to the more theoretical chapters that have preceded it? How does the faith as experienced in practice illuminate, challenge or enrich the faith as set out earlier in the more detached, sweeping account? Let us briefly review the earlier claims through the lens of these historical narratives.

Faith is first about the Triune God revealed in Jesus. While sometimes submerged or obscured in cultural assumptions or institutional sclerosis, this central claim is as undisputed today as at any time in the history of the Church of England and the Anglican Communion. Perhaps only in the late eighteenth century, when some clergy in England, the United States and elsewhere had come to suppose preaching was largely about edifying wisdom and civilizing ethics, has this central tenet ever been in serious jeopardy.

Faith is about the Jews. This has been easier to forget. At times, both English and American believers have come to assume that their own nation has taken on the mantle of Israel, displaying some kind of manifest destiny. At other times, anti-Semitism has lurked overtly or covertly, and the Jewishness of Jesus and the historicity of salvation have been obscured. But remembering and being in relationship with the Jews is about being mindful of the faithfulness of God.

Faith is about the Holy Spirit and the Church. There is no doubt that the shape of the Church – its bishops and sacraments, its worship and mission – has been a preoccupation of Anglicanism, and has often been the form that attention to the incarnation has taken in new lands. This has also led to a widespread involvement in ecumenical dialogue, not always with the assumption that Anglicans should naturally chair the meeting. But in recent decades the charismatic experience of the Holy Spirit has become a highly significant aspect of spirituality in the Anglican Communion, and throughout Anglican history times of revival have continued to stretch Anglican identity and challenge its inclusiveness and flexibility.

Faith is about creation and the kingdom. At its best, Anglicanism has expressed this faith in a concern for every member of every society of which it has become a part. In England this has usually assumed a close relationship with government, although in an increasingly secularized culture the Church of England is needing to demonstrate more subtle ways of embodying its devotion to the well-being of all. In the USA, in a different way in Wales and sometimes in Australia, this has at times developed into a notion of a non-established national Church; but sometimes the trappings of superiority are hard to shed. More recently some Anglicans have expressed this faith in joining a coalition of concern for the planet's ecological balance.

Faith is, finally, about salvation. While much of the attention in recent years concerning the Church in Africa has fallen on conservative understandings of sexuality, perhaps the most significant question the African Churches habitually ask of the rest of the Communion is, 'How much of your idea of salvation is realized today?' The emphasis on healing, on signs of God's living power and on daily dependence on God's providence are, in general, so much more in evidence in the African Churches – and many would say that is precisely a sign that salvation is real and that the kingdom is close at hand. It is surely part of the crisis of the Western Church that it finds it so hard to express what salvation specifically means today – and sometimes even what salvation means eternally – in language that inherits the imagination of the New Testament. Here, perhaps more than anywhere, is where the Churches of the Anglican Communion need each other. As they have always done.

Bibliography

Secondary/General Sources

Allchin, A. M., *Participation in God: A Forgotten Strand in Anglican Tradition*, New York: Morehouse, 1988.

Avis, Paul D. L., *The Anglican Understanding of the Church: An Introduction*, London: SPCK, 2000.

Bartlett, Alan, *A Passionate Balance: The Anglican Tradition*, London: Darton, Longman & Todd, 2007.

Bernardin, Joseph Buchanan, *An Introduction to the Episcopal Church*, 2nd edn, New York: Morehouse-Gorham, 1955.

Chapman, Mark D., *Anglicanism: A Very Short Introduction*, Oxford; New York: Oxford University Press, 2006.

Dormor, Duncan J., Jack McDonald and Jeremy Caddick, *Anglicanism: The Answer to Modernity*, London; New York: Continuum, 2003.

Elgin, Kathleen, *The Episcopalians: The Protestant Episcopal Church*, New York: D. McKay, 1971.

Greer, Rowan A., *Anglican Approaches to Scripture: From the Reformation to the Present*, New York: Crossroad, 2006.

Griffiss, James E., *The Anglican Vision*, Cambridge, MA: Cowley, 1997.

Hein, David and Gardiner H. Shattuck, *The Episcopalians*, Westport, CT: Praeger, 2004.

Holloway, Richard, *The Anglican Tradition*, London: Mowbray, 1984.

Holmes, Urban Tigner, *What Is Anglicanism?*, Wilton, CT: Morehouse-Barlow, 1982.

Howe, John W. and Samuel C. Pascoe, *Our Anglican Heritage: Can an Ancient Church Be a Church of the Future?*, 2nd edn, Eugene, OR: Cascade, 2010.

O'Donovan, Oliver, *On the Thirty Nine Articles: A Conversation with Tudor Christianity*, Exeter: Paternoster, 1986.

Pittenger, W. Norman, *The Episcopalian Way of Life*, Englewood Cliffs, NJ: Prentice-Hall, 1957.

Sykes, Stephen, *The Integrity of Anglicanism*, New York: Seabury, 1978.

—— *Unashamed Anglicanism*, Nashville, TN: Abingdon, 1995.

Williams, Rowan, *Anglican Identities*, Cambridge, MA: Cowley, 2003.

Wilmer, William H., *The Episcopal Manual*, 3rd edn, Baltimore, MD: E. J. Coale, 1829.

Primary Sources (by Chapter)

Chapter 1: The Faith

Bell, G. K. A., *Christian Unity: The Anglican Position*, Olaus Petri Lectures at Upsala University, October 1946, London: Hodder & Stoughton, 1948.

Church of England, *The Mystery of Salvation: The Story of God's Gift: A Report*, Harrisburg, PA: Morehouse, 1995.

Farrer, Austin Marsden, *Saving Belief: a Discussion of Essentials*, Hodder & Stoughton, 1964.

Gladstone, William, *Church Principles Considered in Their Results*, London: John Murray, Hatchard, 1840.

Gore, Charles, *The Incarnation of the Son of God: Being the Bampton Lectures for the Year 1891*, London: John Murray, 1891.

—— *Lux Mundi: A Series of Studies in the Religion of the Incarnation*, London: John Murray, 1890.

Greene-McCreight, K. E., 'The Only Son of God', in *The Rule of Faith: Scripture, Canon and Creed in a Critical Age*, ed. Ephraim Radner and George Sumner, Harrisburg, PA: Morehouse, 1998, pp. 27–35.

Jewel, John, *An Apology of the Church of England*, Ithaca, NY: Cornell University Press, 1963.

Pobee, John S., 'An African Anglican's View of Salvation', in *Anglicanism: A Global Communion*, ed. Andrew Wingate, et al., London: Mowbray, 1998, pp. 78–84.

Quash, Ben, 'The Anglican Church as a Polity of Presence', in *Anglicanism: The Answer to Modernity*, ed. Duncan Dormer, Jack McDonald and Jeremy Caddick, London; New York: Continuum, 2003, pp. 38–57.

Ramsey, Michael, *Holy Spirit: A Biblical Study*, London: SPCK, 1977.

Simeon, Charles, *Evangelical Preaching*, Portland, OR: Multnomah, 1986.

Stott, John R. W., *Basic Christianity*, Grand Rapids, MI: Eerdmans, 2008.

Tanner, Kathryn, *God and Creation in Christian Theology*, Minneapolis, MN: Fortress, 2005.

Taylor, Barbara Brown, *Speaking of Sin: The Lost Language of Salvation*, Cambridge, MA: Cowley, 2000.

Traherne, Thomas and Denise Inge, *Happiness and Holiness: Thomas Traherne and His Writings*, Norwich: Canterbury Press, 2008.

Wiles, Maurice F., *Faith and the Mystery of God*, Philadelphia: Fortress, 1982.

Chapter 2: The Sources of the Faith

Butler, Joseph, *The Analogy of Religion*, New York: F. Ungar, 1961.

Dix, Gregory, *The Shape of the Liturgy*, London; New York: Continuum, 2005.

Greer, Rowan A., *Anglican Approaches to Scripture: From the Reformation to the Present*, New York: Crossroad, 2006.

Hooker, Richard, *Of the Laws of Ecclesiastical Polity*, abridged, ed. A. S. McGrade and Brian Vickers, New York: St. Martin's Press, 1975.

Hoskyns, Edwyn Clement, *The Riddle of the New Testament*, 3rd edn, London: Faber & Faber, 1947.

Ndungane, Njongonkulu, 'Scripture: What is at Issue in Anglicanism Today?', in *Beyond Colonial Anglicanism*, ed. Ian Douglas and Kwok Pui-Lan, New York: Church Publishing, 2001, pp. 233–46.

Newman, John Henry, *Tracts for the Times*, London: J. G. F. & J. Rivington; Oxford: J. H. Parker, 1840.

Radner, Ephraim, 'The Scriptural Community: Authority in Anglicanism', in *The Fate of Communion: The Agony of Anglicanism and the Future of a Global Church*, ed. Ephraim Radner and Philip Turner, Grand Rapids, MI: Eerdmans, 2006, pp. 90–112.

Robinson, John A. T., *Honest to God*, Philadelphia: Westminster, 1963.

Seitz, Christopher, 'Creed, Scripture, and "Historical Jesus"', in *The Rule of Faith*, ed. Ephraim Radner and George Sumner, Harrisburg, PA: Morehouse, 1998, pp. 126–35.

Tindal, Matthew, *Christianity as Old as the Creation*, Faksimile-Neudruck der Ausgabe London 1730, Stuttgart-Bad Cannstatt: Frommann-Holzboog, 1967.

Westcott, Brooke Foss, *The Bible in the Church: A Popular Account of the Collection and Reception of the Holy Scriptures in the Christian Churches*, London: Macmillan, 1913.

Chapter 3: The Order of the Faith

Bolt, Peter, 'Interpreting Australian Society for Christian Mission', in *'Wonderful and Confessedly Strange': Australian Essays in Anglican*

Ecclesiology, ed. Bruce Norman Kaye, Sarah Macneil and Heather Thomson, Hindmarsh, S. Aust: ATF Press, 2006, pp. 293–313.

Chiwanga, Simon E., 'Beyond the Monarch/Chief: Reconsidering the Episcopacy in Africa', in *Beyond Colonial Anglicanism*, ed. Ian Douglas and Kwok Pui-Lan, New York: Church Publishing, 2001, pp. 297–317.

Coakley, Sarah, 'Prayer, Place and the Poor', in *Praying for England: Priestly Presence in Contemporary Culture*, ed. Samuel Wells and Sarah Coakley, London; New York: Continuum, 2008, pp. 1–20.

Hooker, Richard, *Of the Laws of Ecclesiastical Polity*, abridged, ed. A. S. McGrade and Brian Vickers, New York: St Martin's, 1975.

Jefferts Schori, Katharine, *A Wing and a Prayer: A Message of Faith and Hope*, Harrisburg, PA: Morehouse, 2007.

Jenkins, Timothy, 'Anglicanism: The Only Answer to Modernity', in *Anglicanism: The Answer to Modernity*, ed. Duncan Dormer, Jack McDonald and Jeremy Caddick, London; New York: Continuum, 2003, pp. 186–205.

Okorocha, Cyril, 'Evangelism in the Anglican Communion', in *Anglicanism: A Global Communion*, ed. Andrew Wingate, London: Mowbray, 1998, pp. 323–30.

Stringfellow, William, *My People Is the Enemy: An Autobiographical Polemic*, New York: Holt, Rinehart & Winston, 1964.

Underhill, Evelyn, *The Mystery of Sacrifice: A Meditation on the Liturgy*, London; New York: Longmans, Green & Co., 1938.

Venn, Henry, *To Apply the Gospel: Selections from the Writings of Henry Venn*, Grand Rapids, MI: Eerdmans, 1971.

Williams, Rowan, 'Being a People: Reflections on the Concept of the "Laity"', *Religion, State and Society* 27/1 (1999), pp. 11–21.

Chapter 4: The Character of the Faith

Chase, Philander, *Reminisces: An Autobiography*, Vol. 1, 2nd edn, Boston: James B. Dow, 1848.

Church of the Province of New Zealand, *A New Zealand Prayer Book*, Auckland: Collins, 1989.

Hassett, Miranda Katherine, *Anglican Communion in Crisis: How Episcopal Dissidents and Their African Allies Are Reshaping Anglicanism*, Princeton: Princeton University Press, 2007.

Maurice, Frederick Denison and J. N. Morris, *To Build Christ's Kingdom: F. D. Maurice and His Writings*, London: Canterbury Press, 2007.

Mbiti, John S., *Bible and Theology in African Christianity*, Nairobi: Oxford University Press, 1986.

Okeke, Ken, 'The Anglican Debate in West Africa on Christian-Muslim Relations', in *Anglicanism: A Global Communion*, ed. Andrew Wingate et al., London: Mowbray, 1998, pp. 316–23.

Prichard, Robert W., 'The Place of Doctrine in the Episcopal Church', in *Reclaiming Faith: Essays on Orthodoxy in the Episcopal Church and the Baltimore Declaration*, ed. Ephraim Radner and George R. Sumner, Grand Rapids, MI: Eerdmans, 1993, pp. 13–45.

Seabury, Samuel and Anne W. Rowthorn, *Miles to Go before I Sleep: Samuel Seabury's Journal from 1791–1795*, Hartford, CT: Church Missions, 1982.

Selvanayagam, Israel, 'Anglicans and Inter-Faith Relations – a Historical Retrospect', in *Anglicanism: A Global Communion*, ed. Andrew Wingate et al., London: Mowbray, 1998, pp. 341–6.

Temple, William, *Christianity and Social Order*, New York: Penguin, 1942.

Tutu, Desmond and John Webster, *Crying in the Wilderness: The Struggle for Justice in South Africa*, 3rd edn, London: Mowbray, 1990.

Vanstone, W. H., *Love's Endeavour, Love's Expense: The Response of Being to the Love of God*, London: Darton, Longman & Todd, 1977.

Ward, Kevin, *A History of Global Anglicanism*, Cambridge; New York: Cambridge University Press, 2006.

White, William, 'Case of the Episcopal Churches', in *Readings from the History of the Episcopal Church*, ed. Robert W. Prichard, Wilton, CT: Morehouse-Barlow, 1986, pp. 58–80.

Wilberforce, William, *Christianity and Politics*, Washington, DC: Family Research Council, 2004.

Appendix 1

Thirty Nine Articles of Religion[22]

1. Of Faith in the Holy Trinity.
There is but one living and true God, everlasting, without body, parts,
or passions; of infinite power, wisdom, and goodness; the Maker, and
Preserver of all things both visible and invisible. And in unity of this
Godhead there be three Persons, of one substance, power, and eternity;
the Father, the Son, and the Holy Ghost.

2. Of the Word or Son of God, which was made very Man.
The Son, which is the Word of the Father, begotten from everlasting
of the Father, the very and eternal God, and of one substance with the
Father, took Man's nature in the womb of the blessed Virgin, of her
substance: so that two whole and perfect Natures, that is to say, the
Godhead and Manhood, were joined together in one Person, never to
be divided, whereof is one Christ, very God, and very Man; who truly
suffered, was crucified, dead, and buried, to reconcile his Father to us,
and to be a sacrifice, not only for original guilt, but also for actual sins
of men.

3. Of the going down of Christ into Hell.
As Christ died for us, and was buried, so also is it to be believed, that
he went down into Hell.

4. Of the Resurrection of Christ.
Christ did truly rise again from death, and took again his body, with
flesh, bones, and all things appertaining to the perfection of Man's
nature; wherewith he ascended into Heaven, and there sitteth, until he
return to judge all Men at the last day.

---

22 Source: http://www.anglicancommunion.org/resources/acis/docs/thirty_
nine_articles.cfm

5. Of the Holy Ghost.

The Holy Ghost, proceeding from the Father and the Son, is of one substance, majesty, and glory, with the Father and the Son, very and eternal God.

6. Of the Sufficiency of the Holy Scriptures for Salvation.

Holy Scripture containeth all things necessary to salvation: so that whatsoever is not read therein, nor may be proved thereby, is not to be required of any man, that it should be believed as an article of the Faith, or be thought requisite or necessary to salvation. In the name of the Holy Scripture we do understand those canonical Books of the Old and New Testament, of whose authority was never any doubt in the Church.

Of the Names and Number of the Canonical Books.

- Genesis
- Exodus
- Leviticus
- Numbers
- Deuteronomy
- Joshua
- Judges
- Ruth
- The First Book of Samuel
- The Second Book of Samuel
- The First Book of Kings
- The Second Book of Kings
- The First Book of Chronicles
- The Second Book of Chronicles
- The First Book of Esdras
- The Second Book of Esdras
- The Book of Esther
- The Book of Job
- The Psalms
- The Proverbs
- Ecclesiastes or Preacher
- Cantica, or Songs of Solomon
- Four Prophets the greater
- Twelve Prophets the less.

And the other Books (as Hierome saith) the Church doth read for example of life and instruction of manners; but yet doth it not apply them to establish any doctrine; such are these following:

- The Third Book of Esdras
- The Fourth Book of Esdras
- The Book of Tobias
- The Book of Judith
- The rest of the Book of Esther
- The Book of Wisdom
- Jesus the Son of Sirach
- Baruch the Prophet
- The Song of the Three Children
- The Story of Susanna
- Of Bel and the Dragon
- The Prayer of Manasses
- The First Book of Maccabees
- The Second Book of Maccabees

All the Books of the New Testament, as they are commonly received, we do receive, and account them Canonical.

7. Of the Old Testament.
The Old Testament is not contrary to the New: for both in the Old and New Testament everlasting life is offered to Mankind by Christ, who is the only Mediator between God and Man, being both God and Man. Wherefore they are not to be heard, which feign that the old Fathers did look only for transitory promises. Although the Law given from God by Moses, as touching Ceremonies and Rites, do not bind Christian men, nor the Civil precepts thereof ought of necessity to be received in any commonwealth; yet notwithstanding, no Christian man whatsoever is free from the obedience of the Commandments which are called Moral.

8. Of the Creeds.
The Three Creeds, Nicene Creed, Athanasius' Creed, and that which is commonly called the Apostles' Creed, ought thoroughly to be received and believed: for they may be proved by most certain warrants of Holy Scripture.

9. Of Original or Birth-Sin.
Original sin standeth not in the following of Adam, (as the Pelagians do vainly talk;) but it is the fault and corruption of the Nature of every man, that naturally is engendered of the offspring of Adam; whereby man is very far gone from original righteousness, and is of his own nature inclined to evil, so that the flesh lusteth always contrary to the Spirit; and therefore in every person born into this world, it deserveth God's wrath and damnation. And this infection of nature doth remain,

yea in them that are regenerated; whereby the lust of the flesh, called in Greek, *phronema sarkos*, (which some do expound the wisdom, some sensuality, some the affection, some the desire, of the flesh), is not subject to the Law of God. And although there is no condemnation for them that believe and are baptized; yet the Apostle doth confess, that concupiscence and lust hath of itself the nature of sin.

10. Of Free-Will.
The condition of Man after the fall of Adam is such, that he cannot turn and prepare himself, by his own natural strength and good works, to faith; and calling upon God. Wherefore we have no power to do good works pleasant and acceptable to God, without the grace of God by Christ preventing us, that we may have a good will, and working with us, when we have that good will.

11. Of the Justification of Man.
We are accounted righteous before God, only for the merit of our Lord and Saviour Jesus Christ by Faith, and not for our own works or deservings. Wherefore, that we are justified by Faith only, is a most wholesome Doctrine, and very full of comfort, as more largely is expressed in the Homily of Justification.

12. Of Good Works.
Albeit that Good Works, which are the fruits of Faith, and follow after Justification, cannot put away our sins, and endure the severity of God's judgment; yet are they pleasing and acceptable to God in Christ, and do spring out necessarily of a true and lively Faith insomuch that by them a lively Faith may be as evidently known as a tree discerned by the fruit.

13. Of Works before Justification.
Works done before the grace of Christ, and the Inspiration of his Spirit, are not pleasant to God, forasmuch as they spring not of faith in Jesus Christ; neither do they make men meet to receive grace, or (as the School-authors say) deserve grace of congruity: yea rather, for that they are not done as God hath willed and commanded them to be done, we doubt not but they have the nature of sin.

14. Of Works of Supererogation.
Voluntary Works besides, over and above, God's Commandments, which they call Works of Supererogation, cannot be taught without arrogancy and impiety: for by them men do declare, that they do not only render unto God as much as they are bound to do, but that they do more for his sake, than of bounden duty is required: whereas Christ saith plainly When ye have done all that are commanded to you, say, We are unprofitable servants.

15. Of Christ alone without Sin.

Christ in the truth of our nature was made like unto us in all things, sin only except, from which he was clearly void, both in his flesh, and in his spirit. He came to be the Lamb without spot, who, by sacrifice of himself once made, should take away the sins of the world; and sin (as Saint John saith) was not in him. But all we the rest, although baptized and horn again in Christ, yet offend in many things; and if we say we have no sin, we deceive ourselves, and the truth is not in us.

16. Of Sin after Baptism.

Not every deadly sin willingly committed after Baptism is sin against the Holy Ghost, and unpardonable. Wherefore the grant of repentance is not to be denied to such as fall into sin after Baptism. After we have received the Holy Ghost, we may depart from grace given, and fall into sin, and by the grace of God we may arise again, and amend our lives. And therefore they are to be condemned, which say, they can no more sin as long as they live here, or deny the place of forgiveness to such as truly repent.

17. Of Predestination and Election.

Predestination to Life is the everlasting purpose of God, whereby (before the foundations of the world were laid) he hath constantly decreed by his counsel secret to us, to deliver from curse and damnation those whom he hath chosen in Christ out of mankind, and to bring them by Christ to everlasting salvation, as vessels made to honour. Wherefore, they which be endued with so excellent a benefit of God, be called according to God's purpose by his Spirit working in due season: they through Grace obey the calling: they be justified freely: they be made sons of God by adoption: they be made like the image of his only-begotten Son Jesus Christ: they walk religiously in good works, and at length, by God's mercy, they attain to everlasting felicity.

As the godly consideration of Predestination, and our Election in Christ, is full of sweet, pleasant, and unspeakable comfort to godly persons, and such as feel in themselves the working of the Spirit of Christ, mortifying the works of the flesh, and their earthly members, and drawing up their mind to high and heavenly things, as well because it doth greatly establish and confirm their faith of eternal Salvation to be enjoyed through Christ as because it doth fervently kindle their love towards God: So, for curious and carnal persons, lacking the Spirit of Christ, to have continually before their eyes the sentence of God's Predestination, is a most dangerous downfall, whereby the Devil doth thrust them either into desperation, or into wretchlessness of most unclean living, no less perilous than desperation.

Furthermore, we must receive God's promises in such wise, as they be generally set forth to us in Holy Scripture: and, in our doings, that Will of God is to be followed, which we have expressly declared unto us in the Word of God.

18. Of obtaining eternal Salvation only by the Name of Christ.

They also are to be had accursed that presume to say, That every man shall be saved by the Law or Sect which he professeth, so that he be diligent to frame his life according to that Law, and the light of Nature. For Holy Scripture doth set out unto us only the Name of Jesus Christ, whereby men must be saved.

19. Of the Church.

The visible Church of Christ is a congregation of faithful men, in which the pure Word of God is preached, and the Sacraments be duly ministered according to Christ's ordinance, in all those things that of necessity are requisite to the same.

As the Church of Jerusalem, Alexandria, and Antioch, have erred, so also the Church of Rome hath erred, not only in their living and manner of Ceremonies, but also in matters of Faith.

20. Of the Authority of the Church.

The Church hath power to decree Rites or Ceremonies, and authority in Controversies of Faith: and yet it is not lawful for the Church to ordain any thing that is contrary to God's Word written, neither may it so expound one place of Scripture, that it be repugnant to another. Wherefore, although the Church be a witness and a keeper of Holy Writ, yet, as it ought not to decree any thing against the same, so besides the same ought it not to enforce any thing to be believed for necessity of Salvation.

21. Of the Authority of General Councils.

General Councils may not be gathered together without the commandment and will of Princes. And when they be gathered together, (forasmuch as they be an assembly of men, whereof all be not governed with the Spirit and Word of God), they may err, and sometimes have erred, even in things pertaining unto God. Wherefore things ordained by them as necessary to salvation have neither strength nor authority, unless it may be declared that they be taken out of holy Scripture.

22. Of Purgatory.

The Romish Doctrine concerning Purgatory, Pardons, Worshipping and Adoration, as well of Images as of Relics, and also Invocation of Saints, is a fond thing, vainly invented, and grounded upon no warranty of Scripture, but rather repugnant to the Word of God.

23. Of Ministering in the Congregation.

It is not lawful for any man to take upon him the office of public preaching, or ministering the Sacraments in the Congregation, before he be lawfully called, and sent to execute the same. And those we ought to judge lawfully called and sent, which be chosen and called to this work by men who have public authority given unto them in the Congregation, to call and send Ministers into the Lord's vineyard.

24. Of Speaking in the Congregation in such a Tongue as the people understandeth.

It is a thing plainly repugnant to the Word of God, and the custom of the Primitive Church to have public Prayer in the Church, or to minister the Sacraments, in a tongue not understood of the people.

25. Of the Sacraments.

Sacraments ordained of Christ be not only badges or tokens of Christian men's profession, but rather they be certain sure witnesses, and effectual signs of grace, and God's good will towards us, by the which he doth work invisibly in us, and doth not only quicken, but also strengthen and confirm our Faith in him.

There are two Sacraments ordained of Christ our Lord in the Gospel, that is to say, Baptism, and the Supper of the Lord.

Those five commonly called Sacraments, that is to say, Confirmation, Penance, Orders, Matrimony, and Extreme Unction, are not to be counted for Sacraments of the Gospel, being such as have grown partly of the corrupt following of the Apostles, partly are states of life allowed in the Scriptures, but yet have not like nature of Sacraments with Baptism, and the Lord's Supper, for that they have not any visible sign or ceremony ordained of God.

The Sacraments were not ordained of Christ to be gazed upon, or to be carried about, but that we should duly use them. And in such only as worthily receive the same, they have a wholesome effect or operation: but they that receive them unworthily, purchase to themselves damnation, as Saint Paul saith.

26. Of the Unworthiness of the Ministers, which hinders not the effect of the Sacraments.

Although in the visible Church the evil be ever mingled with the good, and sometimes the evil have chief authority in the Ministration of the Word and Sacraments, yet forasmuch as they do not the same in their own name, but in Christ's, and do minister by his commission and authority, we may use their Ministry, both in hearing the Word of God, and in receiving the Sacraments. Neither is the effect of Christ's ordinance taken away by their wickedness, nor the grace of God's gifts diminished from such as by faith, and rightly, do receive the Sacraments ministered unto them; which be effectual, because of Christ's institution and promise, although they be ministered by evil men.

Nevertheless, it appertaineth to the discipline of the Church, that inquiry be made of evil Ministers, and that they be accused by those that have knowledge of their offences; and finally, being found guilty, by just judgment be deposed.

27. Of Baptism.
Baptism is not only a sign of profession, and mark of difference, whereby Christian men are discerned from others that be not christened, but it is also a sign of Regeneration or New-Birth, whereby, as by an instrument, they that receive Baptism rightly are grafted into the Church; the promises of the forgiveness of sin, and of our adoption to be the sons of God by the Holy Ghost, are visibly signed and sealed, Faith is confirmed, and Grace increased by virtue of prayer unto God.

The Baptism of young Children is in any wise to be retained in the Church, as most agreeable with the institution of Christ.

28. Of the Lord's Supper.
The Supper of the Lord is not only a sign of the love that Christians ought to have among themselves one to another, but rather it is a Sacrament of our Redemption by Christ's death: insomuch that to such as rightly, worthily, and with faith, receive the same, the Bread which we break is a partaking of the Body of Christ; and likewise the Cup of Blessing is a partaking of the Blood of Christ.

Transubstantiation (or the change of the substance of Bread and Wine) in the Supper of the Lord, cannot be proved by Holy Writ; but is repugnant to the plain words of Scripture, overthroweth the nature of a Sacrament, and hath given occasion to many superstitions.

The Body of Christ is given, taken, and eaten, in the Supper, only after an heavenly and spiritual manner. And the mean whereby the Body of Christ is received and eaten in the Supper, is Faith.

The Sacrament of the Lord's Supper was not by Christ's ordinance reserved, carried about, lifted up, or worshipped.

29. Of the Wicked, which eat not the Body of Christ in the use of the Lord's Supper.

The Wicked, and such as be void of a lively faith, although they do carnally and visibly press with their teeth (as Saint Augustine saith) the Sacrament of the Body and Blood of Christ; yet in no wise are they partakers of Christ: but rather, to their condemnation, do eat and drink the sign or Sacrament of so great a thing.

30. Of both Kinds.

The Cup of the Lord is not to be denied to the Lay-people: for both the parts of the Lord's Sacrament, by Christ's ordinance and commandment, ought to be ministered to all Christian men alike.

31. Of the one Oblation of Christ finished upon the Cross.

The Offering of Christ once made is that perfect redemption, propitiation, and satisfaction, for all the sins of the whole world, both original and actual; and there is none other satisfaction for sin, but that alone. Wherefore the sacrifices of Masses, in the which it was commonly said, that the Priest did offer Christ for the quick and the dead, to have remission of pain or guilt, were blasphemous fables, and dangerous deceits.

32. Of the Marriage of Priests.

Bishops, Priests, and Deacons, are not commanded by God's Law, either to vow the estate of single life, or to abstain from marriage: therefore it is lawful for them, as for all other Christian men, to marry at their own discretion, as they shall judge the same to serve better to godliness.

33. Of excommunicate Persons, how they are to be avoided.

That person which by open denunciation of the Church is rightly cut off from the unity of the Church, and excommunicated, ought to be taken of the whole multitude of the faithful, as an Heathen and Publican, until he be openly reconciled by penance, and received into the Church by a Judge that hath authority thereunto.

34. Of the Traditions of the Church.

It is not necessary that Traditions and Ceremonies be in all places one, or utterly like; for at all times they have been divers, and may be changed according to the diversity of countries, times, and men's manners, so that nothing be ordained against God's Word. Whosoever, through his private judgment, willingly and purposely, doth openly break the Traditions and Ceremonies of the Church, which be not repugnant to the Word of God, and be ordained and approved by common authority, ought to be rebuked openly, (that others may fear to do the like,) as he that offendeth against the common order of the Church, and hurteth the authority of the Magistrate, and woundeth the consciences of the weak brethren.

Every particular or national Church hath authority to ordain, change, and abolish, Ceremonies or Rites of the Church ordained only by man's authority, so that all things be done to edifying.

35. Of the Homilies.

The Second Book of Homilies, the several titles whereof we have joined under this Article, doth contain a godly and wholesome Doctrine, and necessary for these times, as doth the former Book of Homilies, which were set forth in the time of Edward the Sixth; and therefore we judge them to be read in Churches by the Ministers, diligently and distinctly, that they may be understanded of the people.

Of the Names of the Homilies.

- Of the right Use of the Church.
- Against Peril of Idolatry.
- Of repairing and keeping clean of Churches.
- Of good Works, first of Fasting.
- Against Gluttony and Drunkenness.
- Against Excess of Apparel.
- Of Prayer.
- Of the Place and Time of Prayer.
- That Common Prayers and Sacraments ought to be ministered in a known tongue.
- Of the reverent Estimation of God's Word.
- Of Alms-doing.
- Of the Nativity of Christ.
- Of the Passion of Christ.
- Of the Resurrection of Christ.
- Of the worthy receiving of the Sacrament of the Body and Blood of Christ.
- Of the Gifts of the Holy Ghost.
- For the Rogation-days.
- Of the State of Matrimony.
- Of Repentance.
- Against Idleness.
- Against Rebellion.

36. Of Consecration of Bishops and Ministers.

The Book of Consecration of Archbishops and Bishops, and Ordering of Priests and Deacons, lately set forth in the time of Edward the Sixth, and confirmed at the same time by authority of Parliament, doth contain all things necessary to such Consecration and Ordering: neither hath it any thing, that of itself is superstitious and ungodly. And therefore whosoever are consecrated or ordered according to the Rites of that Book, since the second year of the forenamed King Edward unto this time, or hereafter shall be consecrated or ordered according to the same Rites; we decree all such to be rightly, orderly, and lawfully consecrated and ordered.

37. Of the Power of the Civil Magistrates.

The King's Majesty hath the chief power in this Realm of England, and other his Dominions, unto whom the chief Government of all Estates of this Realm, whether they be Ecclesiastical or Civil, in all causes doth appertain, and is not, nor ought to be, subject to any foreign Jurisdiction.

Where we attribute to the King's Majesty the chief government, by which Titles we understand the minds of some slanderous folks to be offended; we give not our Princes the ministering either of God's Word, or of the Sacraments, the which thing the Injunctions also lately set forth by Elizabeth our Queen do most plainly testify; but that only prerogative, which we see to have been given always to all godly Princes in holy Scriptures by God himself; that is, that they should rule all estates and degrees committed to their charge by God, whether they be Ecclesiastical or Temporal, and restrain with the civil sword the stubborn and evil-doers.

The Bishop of Rome hath no jurisdiction in this Realm of England.

The Laws of the Realm may punish Christian men with death, for heinous and grievous offences.

It is lawful for Christian men, at the commandment of the Magistrate, to wear weapons, and serve in the wars.

38. Of Christian Men's Goods, which are not common.

The Riches and Goods of Christians are not common, as touching the right, title, and possession of the same; as certain Anabaptists do falsely boast. Notwithstanding, every man ought, of such things as he possesseth, liberally to give alms to the poor, according to his ability.

39. Of a Christian Man's Oath.

As we confess that vain and rash swearing is forbidden Christian men by our Lord Jesus Christ, and James his Apostle, so we judge, that Christian Religion doth not prohibit, but that a man may swear when the Magistrate requireth, in a cause of faith and charity, so it be done according to the Prophet's teaching in justice, judgement, and truth.

Appendix 2

Lambeth Conference of 1888
Resolution 11[23]

That, in the opinion of this Conference, the following Articles supply a basis on which approach may be by God's blessing made towards Home Reunion:

1 The Holy Scriptures of the Old and New Testaments, as "containing all things necessary to salvation," and as being the rule and ultimate standard of faith.
2 The Apostles' Creed, as the Baptismal Symbol; and the Nicene Creed, as the sufficient statement of the Christian faith.
3 The two Sacraments ordained by Christ Himself--Baptism and the Supper of the Lord--ministered with unfailing use of Christ's words of Institution, and of the elements ordained by Him.
4 The Historic Episcopate, locally adapted in the methods of its administration to the varying needs of the nations and peoples called of God into the Unity of His Church.

---

23 Source: http://www.anglicancommunion.org/resources/acis/docs/chicago_lambeth_quadrilateral.cfm